1584

Nonviolence to Animals, Earth, and Self in Asian Traditions

SUNY Series in Religious Studies
Harold Coward, Editor

Nonviolence to Animals, Earth, and Self in Asian Traditions

Christopher Key Chapple

State University of New York Press

Published by
State University of New York Press, Albany

Printed in the United States of America

For information, address State University of New York
Press, State University Plaza, Albany, NY 12246

Production by Dana Foote
Marketing by Nancy Farrell

Library of Congress Cataloging-in-Publication Data

Chapple, Christopher.
Nonviolence to Animals, Earth, and Self in Asian Traditions /
Christopher Key Chapple.
p. cm. — (SUNY series in religious studies)
Includes bibliographical references and index.
ISBN 0–7914–1497–3 : ISBN 0–7914–1498–1 (pbk.)
1. Nonviolence. 2. Ahiṃsā. 3. Nonviolence—Religious aspects.
4. Passive resistance—Asia. I. Title. II. Series.
HM278.C465 1993
303.6'1—dc20 92–25791
CIP

10 9 8 7 6 5 4 3 2 1

Dedicated to the memory of

Cheryl Ann Wycoff Clary, 1953–1991
and
Kenneth Lee Ketwig, 1954–1991

Contents

issue of Asian nonviolence as a global concept, and prompted me to investigate nonviolent ideas in Western culture.

For the past few years, I have discussed the observance of nonviolence with numerous people. Gurāṇi Añjali, founder and director of Yoga Anand Ashram, provided a daily *sādhana* rooted in *ahiṃsā* and vegetarianism. Richard A. Gard of The Institute for Advanced Studies of World Religions assisted me in my early research into the treatment of animals in Buddhism. Norvin Hein of Yale University helped clarify societal observances of nonviolence in classical Hinduism, which he attributes in part to the small-town atmosphere of village India. Padmanabh S. Jaini of the University of California, Berkeley, inspired me with his writings and stories about Jainism, and encouraged me to visit with Jaina monks in India. John Cort of Denison University helped provide contacts for my journeys to India, as did Purusottama Bilimoria of Deakin University in Australia and Sunil and Naresh Gupta at the Indian Books Centre in Delhi. Y. S. Shastri at Gujerat University, Krishnachand Chordia, a benefactor and student of Jainology at the University of Madras, S. L. Gandhi of Anuvibha in Jaipur, and Sanjeev Shah in Bangalore graciously hosted me during my trip to India in 1989. My visit to Jaina Vishva Bharati in Ladnun was truly remarkable and deeply appreciated, as were my many audiences with Acharya Tulsi. Michael Tobias's film *Ahiṃsā: Nonviolence* and his personal enthusiasm for the Jaina tradition served as a pleasant counterpoint to the more objective approach of most Indological studies. Also of benefit to this project were conversations with James Fitzgerald of the University of Tennessee on the *Mahābhārata*, my colleagues Katherine Harper and Ray Burt at Loyola Marymount University, particularly on the Indus Valley and German materials, respectively, and Jay McDaniel of Hendrix College on theological approaches to environmentalism.

My wife, Maureen, and my children, Dylan and Emma, were very supportive and patient during my trips to India and during the hours I spent at the word processor. Susan Burgerman and Thornton Prime, my research assistants, helped track down various references and assisted in the production of the manuscript, as did my secretary, Carol Turner. Last but not least, I wish to express appreciation to Bill Eastman, who encouraged me to persevere and polish what began as far less than perfect.

Christopher Key Chapple
Loyola Marymount University
Los Angeles, California

Contents

Acknowledgments

A love for animals and the earth, the birth of my two children, and the slow death of two close friends from breast cancer and AIDS prompted me to write this book. It began when the International Association Against Painful Experiments on Animals solicited paper proposals for a conference to be held in England in 1984, organized by Tom Regan. The topic focused on how various religious traditions would respond to the modern practice of using animals in scientific experiments. Having trained in Sanskrit and theology, I decided that it would be interesting to put Indian thought to work on a contemporary ethical issue. My research into Jaina and Buddhist attitudes toward animals, which started during the course of that research in 1984, is continued in this volume. Participation in the National Endowment for the Humanities Summer Seminar on Buddhism and Culture in China and Japan in 1989 at the University of California, Los Angeles, brought me in contact with William LaFleur and Stephen Teiser, who helped locate Chinese and Japanese materials on animals and who also helped develop my conception of the impact of religious ideas on popular culture.

Thomas Berry, the founder of the History of Religions program in the department of theology at Fordham University, rekindled my interest in environmentalism. His example as both teacher and person are reflected in the methodology used in this book, which might be characterized as a combination of cultural, historical, textual, and reflective studies.

Loyola Marymount University provided generous support for my studies of nonviolence in the *Mahābhārata* and in early Jainism. The College Theology Society and the Southern California Seminar on South Asia provided me the opportunity to present my preliminary work on Jaina logic and the fast unto death. The 1989 Margaret Demorest Lectureship and Humanities Festival at Casper College in Wyoming gave me the opportunity to reflect on the issue of Asian nonviolence as a global concept, and prompted me to investigate nonviolent ideas in Western culture.

For the past few years, I have discussed the observance of nonviolence with numerous people. Gurāṇi Añjali, founder and director of Yoga Anand Ashram, provided a daily *sādhana* rooted in *ahiṃsā* and vegetarianism. Richard A. Gard of The Institute for Advanced Studies of World Religions assisted me in my early research into the treatment of animals in Buddhism. Norvin Hein of Yale University helped clarify societal observances of nonviolence in classical Hinduism, which he attributes in part to the small-town atmosphere of village India. Padmanabh S. Jaini of the University of California, Berkeley, inspired me with his writings and stories about Jainism, and encouraged me to visit with Jaina monks in India. John Cort of Denison University helped provide contacts for my journeys to India, as did Purusottama Bilimoria of Deakin University in Australia and Sunil and Naresh Gupta at the Indian Books Centre in Delhi. Y. S. Shastri at Gujerat University, Krishnachand Chordia, a benefactor and student of Jainology at the University of Madras, S. L. Gandhi of Anuvibha in Jaipur, and Sanjeev Shah in Bangalore graciously hosted me during my trip to India in 1989. My visit to Jaina Vishva Bharati in Ladnun was truly remarkable and deeply appreciated, as were my many audiences with Acharya Tulsi. Michael Tobias's film *Ahiṃsā: Nonviolence* and his personal enthusiasm for the Jaina tradition served as a pleasant counterpoint to the more objective approach of most Indological studies. Also of benefit to this project were conversations with James Fitzgerald of the University of Tennessee on the *Mahābhārata*, my colleagues Katherine Harper and Ray Burt at Loyola Marymount University, particularly on the Indus Valley and German materials, respectively, and Jay McDaniel of Hendrix College on theological approaches to environmentalism.

My wife, Maureen, and my children, Dylan and Emma, were very supportive and patient during my trips to India and during the hours I spent at the word processor. Susan Burgerman and Thornton Prime, my research assistants, helped track down various references and assisted in the production of the manuscript, as did my secretary, Carol Turner. Last but not least, I wish to express appreciation to Bill Eastman, who encouraged me to persevere and polish what began as far less than perfect.

Christopher Key Chapple
Loyola Marymount University
Los Angeles, California

A Note on Diacritical Marks

For the Sanskrit materials, standard Romanization of the Devanagari script is employed, except in quotations. For East Asian languages, the style of transliteration follows what has been provided by the source cited.

Introduction

This book sets out to explore the practice of nonviolence as defined in the Asian context. In Western cultures, nonviolence usually denotes passive, nonresistant civil disobedience, pacifism, and conscientious objection to war. It is associated particularly with the Christian teachings of the Religious Society of Friends (Quakers) and other radical reform movements that rely on Biblical injunctions to "love your neighbor as yourself" and to "turn the other cheek." In India, nonviolence is referred to as *ahimsā* and is most closely associated with the Jaina religion. It is a personal commitment to respect life in its myriad forms. Its most notable application comes in the form of vegetarianism, universally observed by Jainas, and selectively observed by Hindus, particularly of the Brahmin caste, and Chinese Buddhist monks.

The first part of the book, comprising the first three chapters, focuses on the origins and history of *ahimsā*, its spread from India into East Asia, and specific forms of nonviolent practice that can be applied to two modern issues: animal rights and protection of the environment. The second part of the book turns inward, considering how the nonviolent perspective can influence one's thinking about others and about death.

The opening chapter of the book considers the origins of *ahimsā* in ancient India, with particular attention given to the Jaina tradition. It advances the thesis that the practice of nonviolence arose from an ancient renouncer tradition that later gave birth to Jainism and Buddhism and heavily influenced aspects of Hinduism, including the classical yoga school. As part of this investigation of origins, the fully developed classical Jaina tradition is discussed.

The second chapter traces the spread of this concept with the Buddhist tradition into China and Japan, where stories of animal protection and advocacy of vegetarianism take on dramatic flair. Some implications that Buddhist and Jaina treatment of animals hold for the contemporary issue of animal rights are also discussed.

The third chapter, based in part on my travels within India, probes how Asian approaches to nonviolence might help inform the newly emerging field of environmental ethics. It includes references to Hindu feminist environmentalism, and to the possible interface between Gaia theory and Jaina cosmology.

In the second section of the book, models for a nonviolent self are explored, beginning with a reflective essay on one of the greatest war epics ever composed: the *Mahābhārata*. The interplay of self and otherness is examined as a foundation for understanding both violence and nonviolence. When other stands opposed to self, violence can proceed. When other is seen as self, nonviolence can prevail.

The next chapter discusses the perspectival logic of the Jainas as an expression of nonviolence. In contrast to dualistic assessments of reality that emphasize good and bad, positive and negative, heaven and hell, Jainism offers a sevenfold view. In this chapter, a comparison is made between the Jaina critique of other religious traditions and the modern field of interreligious dialogue. The multivalent, nondogmatic approach found in the *Bhagavad Gītā* and *Yoga Sūtra* is also discussed as a model for nonjudgmental, nonviolent thinking.

In the third essay of this section, the Jaina fast unto death is discussed in relation to the practice of nonviolence. In light of Jaina cosmology and lifestyle, this observance provides an intriguing alternative to modern medicine's tendency to prolong life.

In each of these three essays, the self is seen in light of nonviolence, first by seeing self as other, next by expanding the categories through which one assesses reality, and finally by not clinging to life when its demise cannot be avoided.

The concluding chapter discusses some parallel approaches to nonviolence found in Western culture.

This book examines nonviolence from a variety of perspectives. It is both historical and constructive. It is suggested here that the ethical challenge posed by *ahiṃsā* can help address issues of contemporary life, such as the abuse of animals, the current state of ecological ravage, and the disconnectedness and dehumanization of mass society. A system such as *ahiṃsā*, which originates from outside the structures of science and technology, might help inform or perhaps inspire new models for personal and societal reform.

Part I

Nonviolence, Animals, and Earth

Chapter 1

Origins and Traditional Articulations of Ahiṃsā

The concept of *ahiṃsā* or nonviolence as it developed in India is closely linked with notions of karma. In the context of the *Ṛg Veda*, karma means ritual action; through one's actions in the sacrificial process, certain benefits are said to be assured. Numerous studies of early Hindu notions of karma as summarized in Herman Tull's *The Vedic Origins of Karma*, and my earlier study of karma (*Karma and Creativity*) establish a link between Vedic ritual action and Upaniṣadic forms of meditative transformation.[1] However, although such Vedic sources as the *Śatapatabrāhmaṇa*, and the *Chāndogya* and *Bṛhadāraṇyaka Upaniṣads* make mention of the efficacy of ritual action in creating and maintaining the world in which one lives, these texts from the earliest phases of Hindu thought do not demonstrate as great an emphasis on ethics as expressed in later Hindu texts that list nonviolence as preeminent. The earliest mention of the ethical importance of karma in the Hindu context is found in the *Bṛhadāraṇyaka Upaniṣad*, when Yājñavalkya states that "one becomes good by good action, bad by bad" (3.2.10.13). It is only in the later *Dharmaśāstra* materials that the specific doctrine of rebirth according to one's meritorious or sinful deeds is fully expounded.[2]

Within the very first written documents of the Jaina tradition, by contrast, we see a fully developed and quite distinct doctrine of karma that entails strict observance of ethical precepts rooted in *ahiṃsā*. The earliest extant text of the Jainas, the *Ācārāṅga Sūtra*, dating from the fourth century B.C.E., proclaims a much stronger message than that of Yājñavalkya:

> Injurious activities inspired by self-interest lead to evil and darkness. This is what is called bondage, delusion, death, and hell. To do harm to others is to do harm to oneself. "Thou art he whom thou intendest to kill! Thou art he whom thou intendest to tyrranize over!" We corrupt ourselves as soon as we intend to corrupt others. We kill ourselves as soon as we intend to kill others.[3]

As we will see, the ideas contained in this passage found full development in the cosmology and psychology of the Jaina tradition. We also will see parallel developments in Hinduism, though the practice of animal sacrifice, inseparable from the all-important Vedic ritual tradition, mitigates the extent to which Hindus can be said to embrace fully the doctrine of *ahiṃsā*.

Before we turn to an examination of the theory and practice of *ahiṃsā* in the classical texts of Jainism and Hinduism, two other topics need to be addressed. First, in order to place the present study in the context of modern scholarship on this topic, a brief survey will be given of previous work on the origins of *ahiṃsā*. Second, we will discuss the possible archaic origins of Jainism in the Indus Valley civilization. Although any discussion of this early phase of India is difficult to undertake, due to the lack of translated textual materials, various scholars have suggested that certain artifacts of the Indus Valley cities indicate a link with the later Jaina tradition.

A Brief Survey of Prior Studies on the Origins of Ahiṃsā

Modern scholarship has been surprisingly scant and inconclusive on the origins of *ahiṃsā*. Two sources often cited include L. Alsdorf's *Beiträge zur Geschichte von Vegetarismus und Rinderverehrung in Indien*,[4] and Hanns-Peter Schmidt's "The Origin of *Ahiṃsā*." Both of these studies emphasize social law theory as found in Hindu law manuals. Although they mention Jaina nonviolence, they seem to minimize its importance; Schmidt states that "the concept of ahiṃsā as we meet it with the Jainas is not based on ethical ideas but on a magico-ritualistic dread of destroying life in any form."[5] These authors also claim that Mahāvīra, the organizer of what has become institutional Jainism, was not a vegetarian, a claim that has been contradicted by Jaina scholar H. R. Kapadia.[6]

Alsdorf and Schmidt differ sharply on the extent to which the Indus Valley culture may have contributed to later Indian religions. Alsdorf suggests that Śiva worship, reincarnation, veneration of the cow, and nonviolence all have roots in Indus Valley culture. Schmidt dismisses the notion that vegetarianism is found in the Indus Valley civilization, stating that these people could not have been vegetarian because the bones of flesh animals were found in the ruins of Mohenjodaro and Harappa. He writes that "there are...no traces of similar ideas to be found among the non-Aryan population of India—not influenced by the Brahmanical culture—which could justify the assumption that *ahiṃsā* and vegetarianism did not originate from conceptions evolved among the Aryans."[7] Recent scholarly investigations tend to refute Schmidt's conclusions, as materials in the next section indicate. Additionally, I would like to suggest that the presence of bones in a city's garbage does not mean that all its inhabitants ate meat. Within India to the present day, both carnivores and vegetarians coexist. Although the articles by Schmidt and Alsdorf are often cited as the standard studies on the origins of nonviolence, they do not seem to pay sufficient attention to the Jaina texts, particularly the *Ācārāṅga Sūtra*, which, having been composed in the fourth or early third century B.C.E.,[8] predates the Hindu *Dharmaśāstra* material upon which these authors base most of their arguments.

Other materials on the history and literature of *ahiṃsā* include Unto Tahtinen's *Ahiṃsā: Nonviolence in Indian Tradition*,[9] which provides an anthology of select texts on the topic, with emphasis on the Brahmanical tradition. An article by Carlo della Casa discusses the original philosophical impetus of nonviolent perspectives, drawing primarily from later Jaina and Mahayana Buddhist sources.[10] Peter Schreiner examines the issue of nonviolence as presented in a dialogue between Bhīṣma and Yudhiṣṭhira in the *Śāntiparvan* of the *Mahābhārata*.[11] Koshelya Walli provides a comprehensive survey of nonviolence in India that is particularly useful to those interested in Gandhian studies. She elucidates its impetus from classical sources up into the present.[12] Wilhelm Halbfass investigates the Mīmāṃsā defense of animal sacrifice in face of resistance from advocates of *ahiṃsā*,[13] a debate that occurs in the seventh century C.E. In summary, the body of scholarship on the origins of nonviolence is largely restricted to a discussion of Hindu texts, with occasional reference to select Jaina materials.

Possible Indus Valley Origin of the Jaina Tradition

Archaeological evidence of cities dated as early as 3000 B.C.E. points to the presence of a civilization in the Indus Valley characterized by orderly cities and extensive use of terracotta seals. From the layout of the cities, it has been hypothesized that the civilization was remarkably stable, exhibiting virtually no change for a period of over a thousand years. The standardized building materials, the extensive plumbing and drainage systems, and the sturdiness of the ruins at Mohenjodaro, Harappa, Lothal, and elsewhere, give witness to the durablility of a remarkable society, one of sufficient sophistication to engage in trade with the Sumerians and the Egyptians. However, streets and bricks give little insight regarding the hearts and minds of the Indus Valley peoples. For this we turn to the terracotta seals, the interpretation of which has prompted a great deal of speculation and a fair amount of controversy.

The seals of the Indus Valley civilization, many of which can be examined closely at the British Museum, measure approximately two inches by two inches, and depict a variety of scenes: a meditating proto-yogi or proto-Śiva; several depictions of adorned bulls; meditating figures surrounded by animals; and representations of women, both in the seals and in numerous amulets. Asko Parpola has written that these "mostly realistic pictures of animals" denote that they were "apparently worshipped as sacred."[14]

Several scholars, including Ramprasad Chandra, John Marshall, and Mircea Eliade, claim that current yogic practices stem from Indus Valley shamanistic rituals as indicated on these seals. However, Doris Srinivasan warns against associating them with later Hindu culture. Rather than assenting to the theory that the yogins depicted in the various seals are in fact early versions of the Hindu god Śiva, she suggests that "the figure represents a divine bull-man, possibly a deity of fertility and abundance."[15] However, she does not dispute the notion that approximations of yoga postures are represented on the seals. Jean Filiozat and Hanns-Peter Schmidt claim that yoga was not related to indigenous cultures but scientifically developed by the Aryan invaders of India.[16] This thesis rests on the assumption that the Indus Valley people were in fact conquered by the Aryans, also known as Indo-Europeans, a notion that has recently been challenged by Colin Renfrew.[17] Renfrew notes that the seals found in Mohenjodaro and Harappa were also found near the Caspian sea and suggests that "early Indo-European languages were spoken in North India by the sixth millennium B.C."[18]

Both the meditative poses and the apparent veneration for animals have been cited by Thomas McEvilley as evidence of a proto-yoga tradition in India, akin to Jainism. In support of his claim, he refers to the Indus seal wherein various animals surround a person engaged in what he describes as *mūlabandhāsana*, a sitting yogic pose wherein one's heels are pressed against the perineum with knees pressed firmly to the ground. McEvilley links this figure with the totem and taboo practices described by anthropologists.[19] In shamanic initiation, the practitioner receives training in the art of taking on the powers of a particular animal; in some societies, a clan or even an unrelated group of people will devote themselves to a particular animal. That animal becomes sacred and will not be killed by members of the group, though other animals might be used for food.

This particular image, depicting a contemplative figure surrounded by a multitude of animals might suggest that perhaps all the animals depicted are sacred to this particular practitioner. Consequently these animals would be protected from harm. This might be the first indication of the practice of *ahiṃsā*.

This particular scene is also described in the *Ācārāṅga Sūtra*, the oldest text of the Jaina canon. It is said to adorn the palanquin that Mahāvīra ascended in the fantastic and embellished tale that describes his renunciation. Śakra, the leader and king of the gods, praises, worships, and annoints him for his decision to leave the world; he clads Mahāvīra in beautiful robes "interwoven with gold and ornamented with designs of flamingos," adorns him with necklaces, a turban, wreaths of precious stones, ribbons, and more. He then creates a giant palanquin

> adorned with pictures of wolves, bulls, horses, men, dolphins, birds, monkeys, elephants, antelopes, *sarabhas* (fantastic animals with eight legs), yaks, tigers, lions, [and] creepings plants.[20]

This scene with its great variety of creatures is like that found in the Indus Valley seals and echoed in later Indian iconography as well. It can be interpreted as depicting harmony within nature and, I might add, it could provide early indication of reverence for all living beings.

McEvilley offers various other evidence for a possible link between the Indus Valley culture and later institutional forms of Jainism. Seal 420, unearthed at Mohenjodaro, portrays a person with three or possibly four faces. Jaina iconography frequently depicts its *Tīrthaṅkaras* with four faces, symbolizing their missionary activity in all four directions.[21] The figure portrayed in seal 420, as well as those depicted in seals 222 and 235 and in various other images, sits in the *mūlabandhāsana* mentioned above. According to McEvilley, the first literary mention of this pose is found in the *Ācārāṅga Sūtra* and then repeated in the *Kalpa Sūtra* in association with Mahāvīra's pose when he entered into the state of *kevala*, the pinnacle of Jaina spirituality:

> ...under a Sal tree,...in a squatting position with joined heels, exposing himself to the heat of the sun, after fasting two and a half days without drinking water, being engaged in deep meditation, [Mahāvīra] reached the highest knowledge and intuition, called Kevala, which is infinite, supreme, unobstructed, unimpeded, complete, and full.[22]

For McEvilley, the depiction of this pose in the Indus Valley materials and its later description in Jaina texts provides strong evidence of a link between archaic and institutional religion in India. However, McEvilley's assumption that Mahāvīra sat in the *mūlabandhāsana* is somewhat contradicted by both the depiction on the seal and by the description found in the texts. On the seal, it is difficult to clearly ascertain if the knees are firmly planted on the ground, which is essential for *mūlabandhāsana* as traditionally practiced. In the text, the pose is described as a squatting position, known as the *godoha-āsana* or cow-milking pose.[23] This differs from McEvilley's naming of the pose, but does resemble the position as drawn on the seal.

One stamped amulet from Mohenjodaro depicts a figure in what McEvilley calls *mūlabandhāsana* flanked by two devotees and two upright serpents; McEvilley notes that the Tīrthaṅkara Pārśvanatha, at the moment he passed into *kevala*, was "protected on both sides by upright serpents."[24] Pārśvanatha has been verified as living around the time of 850 B.C.E. The seal is presumably older, but may indicate a stylistic tradition associated with spiritual accomplishment that was passed down through the centuries.

Another seal depicts seven persons in "an upright posture with arms hanging somewhat stiffly and held slightly away from the sides of the body," which McEvilley correlates with the Jaina *kāyotsarga* pose, the posture in which the very first Tīrthaṅkara, Ṛṣabha, is said to have entered *kevala.*[25] The particular seal used for this argument is elsewhere interpreted in so many different ways that this would be very difficult to establish. This seal has been used also in an attempt to establish the existence of a proto-mother goddess tradition in India.[26] Richard Lannoy, however, does see Jaina influences in this seal: "that of a nude man represented as a repeat-motif in rigidly upright posture, his legs slightly apart, arms held parallel with the sides of his body, which recurs later as the Jaina Tirthankara, repeated row upon row." However, Lannoy also links the same seal to the seven goddesses![27]

Depictions of a bull appear repeatedly in the artifacts of the Indus Valley. Lannoy, McEvilley, and Padmanabh Jaini all have suggested that the abundant use of the bull image in the Indus Valley civilization indicates a link with Ṛṣabha, the first of the twenty four Tīrthaṅkaras, whose companion animal is the bull.[28]

In summary, McEvilley posits that six images indicate a proto-yoga tradition akin to Jainism was present in the Indus Valley: a meditating figure seated in what he calls *mūlabandhāsana*, a similar figure surrounded with an array of benevolent wild animals, a four-faced icon, a meditator flanked by two upright serpents, seven figures in what appears to be the *kāyotsarga* pose, and the bull.

Additionally, the *Ṛg Veda* describes the odd practices of an ancient relgious order wherein men with unshorn locks are described variously as naked, "going where the gods have gone before," intimate with the wind, and "a sweet most delightful friend" (*Ṛg Veda* X:136). The *Atharva Veda* devotes its fifteenth chapter to the Vrātyas, a sect that includes among its practices standing erect in one spot for a full year, a practice mentioned in the *Uttara Sūtra*, a Jaina text. These references to not cutting the hair, postures such as *mūlabandhāsana* and standing motionless, nudity, and so forth, might be indicative of a proto-yogic religion related to later forms of Jainism.

All these materials suggest that some form of religion involving meditation and veneration of animals flourished in the Indus Valley cities. Although it is not possible to conclude that these persons were practitioners of *ahiṃsā* as it exists in its present form, some iconographic and thematic continuity stretching from the Indus Valley into classical and modern Jainism seems evident. We now turn to an investigation of the Jaina religion in its fully developed form, wherein *ahiṃsā* serves as the centerpiece of religious practice.

Ahiṃsā *and the Jaina Religion*

The Jaina and Buddhist traditions are referred to as the heterodox schools of Indian thought. Both reject the authority of the Vedas; both emphasize meditation; both contain teachings regarding rebirth; both were established in their present forms by historical personalities. However, whereas Buddhism is rooted in a markedly anti-theistic stance and generally evades questions of a metaphysical nature, Jainism seemingly combines physics with metaphysics, propounding a world view that regards all aspects of physical reality to be imbued with multitudes of life. This perception of the livingness of things resulted in the practice of *ahiṃsā*, an ethic requiring a respect for all living forms that shaped the day-to-day life of lay Jainas and the austere path followed by Jaina mendicants. This thorough respect for life, and its attendant lifestyle, profoundly influenced Buddhism, Hinduism, and Islam within India and, to the extent that it helped to shape Buddhist practice, spread throughout Asia. We have seen some indications of Jainism's antiquity; a survey of its basic teachings, which have served as a major inspiration for the observance of *ahiṃsā* in India for millenia, now follows.

Jainism is one of the most ancient of India's indigenous traditions, and the oldest of the surviving non-Vedic schools. The name Jainism is derived from the term *jina*, which means conqueror or victor; hence, the Jainas are followers of the path established by the *Jinas*, those who have conquered the suffering (*duḥkha)* inherent in attachment. The most recent Jina, Vardhamāna Mahāvīra, lived from approximately 540 to 468 B.C.E. according to modern scholars; the traditional dates given by Jainas are 599 to 527 B.C.E. His immediate predecessor, Pārśvanatha, has been dated to the years surrounding 850 B.C.E. Twenty-two other Jinas (also known as *Tīrthaṅkaras*) are said to have preceded Mahāvīra and Pārśvanatha, but no historical evidence exists to prove or disprove their existence.

At the heart of Jainism is the practice of *ahiṃsā*, the vow of noninjury. The word *ahiṃsā* comes from the Sanskrit root *hiṃs*, a desiderative form of the verb *han*, to kill or injure or strike. Prefixed with a privative "a," it is best translated as "absence of the desire to kill or harm."[29] This is the prime practice in Jainism for overcoming past actions, and all dimensions of the religion and the philosophy, including its logic, reflect a concern for *ahiṃsā*. Acts of violence are to be avoided because they will result in injury to oneself at some future time, even perhaps in another embodiment. In order to uphold the vows of *ahiṃsā*, two paths of practice were developed: one for the Jaina monks, who adhere to greater vows (*mahāvrata*), and another for the Jaina lay community, who follow a less-rigorous discipline (*aṇuvrata*). These *aṇuvrata* include nonviolence (*ahiṃsā*), truthfulness (*satya*), not stealing (*asteya*), sexual restraint (*brahmacharya*), and nonpossession (*aparigraha*). Four types of violence are acknowledged: intentional, nonintentional, related to profession, and self-defense. The monks live according to rules that avoid all types of violence; lay persons, as we will see, are allowed to take life in some instances. All Jainas are strict vegetarians, living solely on one-sensed beings (vegetables) and milk products. Alcohol, honey, and certain kinds of figs are also prohibited, because they are said to harbor many forms of life, especially *nigoda* (microorganisms).

Ahiṃsā is said to be practiced by the Jaina population, both lay and monastic, in five ways: restraint of mind, control of tongue, carefulness on roads, removing beings from the road, and eating in daylight (to avoid ingesting bugs).[30] In order to observe these forms of *ahiṃsā*, obedience to several rules is enacted to uphold the *aṇuvrata*, including care in movement, speech, eating, placing and removing, and elimination. An additional rule suggests that one limit the area of one's activities, thus renouncing potential harm one may cause in far-off places.[31] This last rule contributes to the regional nature of Jainism: monks face strong prohibitions against travel. These concerns have led the Jaina community to pursue limited means of livelihood: government and farming are acceptable but not desirable occupations; writing, arts, and crafts are encouraged; and commerce is the most desirable, provided that the trade is not conducted in tools of violence, such as in weapons.[32]

For the most advanced monks, the discipline becomes increasingly rigorous. In addition to limited food intake, restraint from sexual desire, and the renunciation of all possessions (in the case of the Digambara sect, any form of clothing is renounced), no digging, bathing, lighting or extinguishing of fires, or fanning is allowed, in order to protect earth, water, fire, and air bodies, respectively.[33]

As evidenced by these prohibitions, the world view of the Jainas presents an unparalleled concern for life. "All beings are fond of life; they like pleasure and hate pain, shun destruction and like to live, they long to live. To all, life is dear."[34] With this basic orientation, the Jaina community has exerted a great deal of influence on Indian society as a whole, though it has consistently remained a tiny minority. They have protested vigorously against the Hindu practice of animal sacrifice. One text declares: "Those terrible ones who kill animals under the guise of making an offering to the gods, or the guise of sacrifice, are bereft of compassion and go to a bad fate."[35] Largely as a result of their efforts, vegetarianism is practiced in all parts of India, and animal sacrifice is now illegal in most states.

The philosophical system underpinning the practice of *ahiṃsā* posits that all being (*sat*) is divided into nonliving (*ajīva*) and living (*jīva*) forms. The nonliving forms include what might be considered principles (motion, rest, space, time) and matter. Matter includes atoms that are indivisible and infinite in number, each possessing form, taste, smell, and palpability. These atoms form the foundation for both physical and psychic or karmic realities.

Within space and continuous with atomic structures are an infinite number of life forces that have existed since beginningless time. The category of living forms includes almost everything regarded as animate or inanimate by non-Jainas. According to Jainism, rocks, mountains, drops of water, lakes, and trees all have life force or *jīva*. These *jīvas* are able to assume diverse dimensions, just as a piece of cloth can be rolled into a small ball or unfolded to occupy an extended space. Each *jīva* is in a state of flux; each is suffused with consciousness (*caitanya*), bliss (*sukha*), and energy (*vīrya*). However, this latter aspect is obscured due to each *jīva* having been defiled by psychic atoms called karma that cause the *jīva* to be reborn repeatedly within a hierarchy of states ranging from that of the gods (*devas*), humans (*manuṣya*), hell beings (*nāraki*), to plants and animals (*tiryañca*), which includes several subcategories. The universe thus conceived is in the shape of a giant person, with hell beings occupying the lower realm, humans and *tiryañca* occupying the middle, gods residing in the heavenly realms which are divided into sixteen abodes, and, finally, dwelling in the *siddha-loka* are the liberated *jīvas* or *kevalins* who have been purged of all karma. This is the final goal, the telos of the cosmos, achieved by those who have successfully and, most likely, repeatedly lived the life of a Jaina monk.

The category of animals and plants (*tiryañca*) is divided into three parts. The lowest form of life is called *nigoda*, beings that "are so undifferentiated that they lack even individual bodies; large clusters of them are born together as colonies which die a fraction of a second later."[36] They are said to reside in flesh, among other places. Above these are the earth bodies, the water bodies, the fire bodies, and the air bodies; these comprise the second group. The third and the highest division of this plant and animal group includes plants and beasts. This entire category is further subdivided into a hierarchy dependent upon the number of senses the life forms possess. The tiny microorganisms known as *nigoda* possess only the sense of touch, as do the earth, water, fire, and air bodies and plant life. Animals are said to possess more than one sense. Worms add the sense of taste; crawling bugs add smell; flies and moths add sight; water serpents add hearing. Mammals, reptiles, fish, and humans all possess six senses, adding mental capacity to the five senses listed above. Gods and hell-beings likewise possess six faculties but also have special powers, arise spontaneously (without parents), and—if a god—continually experience pleasure and—if a demon—experience only anguish. Regardless of one's state of life, from a clod of earth to heavenly beings, repeated existence on the wheel of life is certain until one achieves human birth and begins the quest for liberation.

A *jīva*'s status in this hierarchy is not fixed but is in a constant state of flux, indicated by the Sanskrit term *saṃsāra.* The universe is filled with living beings that have no beginning but that, because of unquenched desires, continually take on new embodiments in one of the four categories (*gati*): gods, humans, hell beings, and animals and plants. We have mentioned that the tradition attributes a thinking faculty (*manas*) to animals; this special ability has spawned the proliferation of numerous stories in which animals make reasoned choices, particularly in regard to nonviolent behavior, that subsequently advance them from animal to human or godly status. One story tells of a frog being trampled by an elephant while en route to hear a lecture by Mahāvīra; he is said to have been reborn in heaven. Similarly, the pair of cobras associated with the Tīrthaṅkara Pārśvanatha were said to have been blessed by him and consequently were reborn in heaven. In a prior birth as a lion, Mahāvīra himself is said to have been so moved by a sermon on the importance of *ahiṃsā* that he refrained from all food normally consumed by a lion, resulting in his death and subsequent human birth wherein he achieved enlightenment. One such story amply demonstrates the Jaina belief that animals can exhibit remarkable powers of both intellect and will:

> Long ago, there was a large forest fire, and all the animals of the forest fled and gathered around a lake, including a herd of elephants, deer, rabbits, squirrels, etc. For hours the animals crowded together in their small refuge, cowering from the fire. The leader of the elephant herd got an itch, and raised a leg to scratch himself. A tiny rabbit quickly occupied the space vacated by the elephant's foot. The elephant, out of an overwhelming desire not to hurt the rabbit, stood on three legs for more than

> three days until the fire died down and the rabbit scampered off. By then, his leg was numb and he toppled over. Still retaining a pure mind and heart, the elephant died. As a reward for his compassion he overcame the need for embodiment as an animal and was born as a prince by the name of Megha and eventually became a disciple of Mahāvīra, taking the vows of a monk in hopes of transcending all forms of existence.[37]

This fanciful story is noteworthy for its confidence in animal abilities, illustrating the Jaina conviction that animals can hold a very high place in the greater order of things.

Under normal circumstances, the most important state to achieve is that of the human being, as this is the only state in which a living being (*jīva*) can be freed totally from the bondage of action (*karma*). For the Jainas, karma is a physical entity, a viscous mass that adheres to the *jīva* and causes attachment and suffering. The average person is filled with karma, which obstructs one's true nature of infinite knowledge, bliss, and energy. The influx (*āsrava*) of new karma must cease if a person is to achieve the pinnacle of all life, the state of liberation, wherein there is no more attachment to passion and impurity. In order to overcome the negative influences of karma, Jainas take on the series of vows mentioned above, the practice of which aids in the purging (*nirjarā*) of the residue accumulated during repeated deleterious activity.

The Jaina tradition presents a highly technical interpretation of karma, considering it to be a material, sticky, colorful substance, composed of atoms, that adheres to the life force and prevents ascent to the *siddha loka*, the world occupied by the liberated ones. This karma is attracted to the *jīva* by acts of violence, and persons who have committed repeated acts of violence are said to be shrouded in a cloud of blackish matter. The following story illustrates the personality type associated with each of the primary five colors (*leśyā*) of karma:

> A hungry person with the most negative black-*leśyā* karma uproots and kills an entire tree to obtain a few mangoes. The person of blue karma fells the tree by chopping the trunk, again merely to gain a handful of fruits. Fraught with grey karma, a third person spares the trunk but cuts off the major limbs of the tree. The one with orangish-red karma carelessly and needlessly lops off several branches to reach the mangoes. The fifth, exhibiting white karma, "merely picks up ripe fruit that has dropped to the foot of the tree."[38]

Through passion, desire, and hatred, the *jīva* attracts karma, which remains until its potency is exhausted. It is stated in the *Sarvārthasiddhi* that the *jīva* "has successively taken in and cast off every particle of karmic matter in the universe." Karma comes in 148 possible forms known as *prakṛtis*, ranging from the destructive (which produces delusions, passions, sentiments and obscurations), to the nondestructive.[39] In the eyes of the Jainas, all karma must be purged (*nirjarā*) in order for liberation to be attained.

The path to liberation in Jainism proceeds through fourteen stages of purification or *guṇasthānas*. At the first stage, *mithyādṛṣṭi*, one suffers from wrong views and is attached to both a sense of self and to things as they appear to be in the world. The second state is similar to the first, but one falls to it after having previously reached a higher state. The third state is transitional, and arises after the second when one begins a reascent to the fourth *guṇasthāna*. In this state, mixture of correct and incorrect views prevails. The fourth state, *samyak darśana*, is pivotal; its significance is second only to the attainment of *Jina* status. It may last from a single instant up to a maximum of forty-eight minutes. In this state, all obstructions of karma are prevented from arising:

> So great is the purity generated by this flash of insight that enormous numbers of bound karmas are driven out of the soul altogether, while future karmic influx is severely limited in both quantity and intensity.[40]

This suppression of karma is preliminary to total elimination, yet it guarantees the *jīva*'s "irreversible entry onto the path that leads to *mokṣa*" (liberation). It heralds a leaving behind of preoccupation with the body, with psychological states, and with possessions. The gross forms of anger, pride, deceit, and greed are "rendered inoperative." One "no longer perceives things as 'attractive' or 'desirable' but one penetrates to the fact that every aspect of life is transitory and mortal."[41] At this point a resolve sets in to change one's lifestyle and to adopt the rigors of Jaina renunciation. Additionally, tremendous compassion arises, wherein all beings are seen as holding the potential to be liberated from the shackles of karma.

It is only after this insight experience that the Jaina lifestyle of *ahiṃsā* is purposefully adopted rather than merely imitated. This happens in the fifth *guṇasthāna*, wherein the vows of a layperson (*aṇuvrata*) are undertaken, which were explained above. Following the "baptism" of insight in the fourth *guṇasthāna*, one undoubtedly has reverted to conventional "wrong views," as indicated in *guṇasthānas* two and three. These disciplines allow the active cultivation of right views on the part of the practitioner, advancing one forward again.

In the subsequent nine stages, increasingly strict monastic vows are adopted, leading to the progressive elimination of karmic matter. First the passions of anger, pride, deceit, and greed are eliminated, not merely suppressed (sixth *guṇasthāna*). Then carelessness is overcome (seventh). Then the subsidiary passions (sentiments) are suppressed. These include laughter, pleasure, displeasure, sorrow, fear, disgust, and sexual cravings (eighth, ninth, tenth). After a hiatus wherein a fall from this state is expected (eleventh), one then proceeds to eliminate any smoldering passions (twelfth), and then the karma that obscures knowledge and perception and restricts energy (thirteenth). In this state, one has become an *arhat*, a *kevalin*, Jina or Tīrthaṅkara. The final (fourteenth) state is obtained the instant before death and signifies the elimination of those karmas that keep one alive (feeling, name, life span, and family).[42] The key to progressing along this path to liberation resides in the observance of *ahiṃsā*, resulting in the progressive purification of the *jīva* through the purging of negative karmic matter.

We have examined the practice of *ahiṃsā* in the Jaina tradition, exploring the greater world view of which it is part, as well as the pathway to liberation with which it is associated. In later chapters, we will return to our discussion of traditional Jainism, with an investigation of its perspectives on logic and its suggestions on how best to approach the end of one's life.

Ahiṃsā *in Hinduism and later Indian Culture*

Having discussed the practices of *ahiṃsā* in the Jaina tradition and some aspects of Jaina thought that support its observance, we now turn to its mention and some of its applications in the Hindu or Brahmanical tradition. At the earliest phase of Hindu culture, *ahiṃsā* is not emphasized. The *Ṛg Veda* mentions *ahiṃsā* only in supplication to Indra for protection from violent enemies. The *Yajur Veda* proclaims: "may all beings look at me with a friendly eye, may I do likewise, and may we look on each other with the eyes of a friend" (36. 18). It is only in the later phase, when the classical form of Hinduism known as Brahmanism begins to emerge, that nonviolence is seen as an important religious value. It may be surmised that this phase of Indian thought, starting around 600 B.C.E., is marked by a merging of traditions; perhaps Śramaṇic or proto-yogic attitudes and influences from Jainism directly influenced Hindu texts and teachings as they developed. One clear example of this process is the adoption of vegetarianism by the Brahman or priestly caste. In the *Ṛg Veda*, Brahmans and others eat meat; by the time of the classical period, vegetarianism becomes a hallmark or indicator of high-caste status.

In the *Chāndogya Upaniṣad*, *ahiṃsā* is mentioned in a list of virtues along with an attribute for one who desires not to "return again." The *Laws of Manu*, which have played a great role in shaping Hindu society, list *ahiṃsā* among the rules to be performed by all castes, along with truthfulness, non-stealing, purity, and control of senses. In regard to meat-eating, the *Laws of Manu*, which date from between 200 B.C.E. and 100 C.E., contain three separate recommendations: that only "kosher" meat may be eaten; that only meat obtained through ritual sacrifice may be eaten; and that one should eat no meat:

> Live on flowers, roots, and fruits alone which are ripened by the time and fallen spontaneously (6. 21). He who for a hundred years annually sacrifices a horse sacrifice and he who does not eat meat [at all]: for both of these the fruit of their meritorious deeds is the same.[43]

As Francis Zimmerman has noted, the *Laws of Manu* contain several strata regarding the status of eating meat because they simultaneously must address the issues of life in the world and renunciation of the world. Meat-eating is traditionally sanctioned in Hinduism as part of the sacrificial process (hence referred to as "kosher") and in emergency situations such as famine.[44] However, greater status is accorded to those who are able to follow a strictly vegetarian diet, prompting Louis Dumont to state that "vegetarianism forced itself on Hindu society, having begun in the sects of the renouncers, among which are Jainism and Buddhism."[45]

The *Mahābhārata*, the great Hindu epic story of the war between two sets of cousins, contains an extensive discussion of the importance of *ahiṃsā*. The following passages attest to the significance of nonviolence within a Hindu context:[46]

> One should never do that to another which one regards as injurious to one's own self. This, in brief, is the rule of *dharma*. Yielding to desire and acting differently, one becomes guilty of *adharma*.
>
> *Mahābhārata* XIII:113. 8

> The meat of other animals is like the flesh of one's son. That foolish person, stupefied by folly, who eats meat, is regarded as the vilest of human beings.
>
> *Mahābhārata* XIII:114:11

> Those high-souled persons who desire beauty, faultlessness of limbs, long life, understanding, mental and physical strength, and memory, should abstain from acts of injury.
>
> *Mahābhārata* XIII:115:8

> Persons endowed with intelligence and purified selves should always behave toward other beings after the manner of that behavior which they like others to observe towards themselves.
>
> *Mahābhārata* XIII:115:22

> *Ahiṃsā* is the *dharma.* It is the highest purification. It is also the highest truth from which all *dharma* proceeds.
>
> *Mahābhārata* XIII:125:25

> *Ahiṃsā* is the highest *dharma. Ahiṃsā* is the best austerity *(tapas). Ahiṃsā* is the greatest gift. *Ahiṃsā* is the highest self control. *Ahiṃsā* is the highest sacrifice. *Ahiṃsā* is the highest power. *Ahiṃsā* is the highest friend. *Ahiṃsā* is the highest truth. *Ahiṃsā* is the highest teaching.
>
> *Mahābhārata* XIII:116:37–41

> The purifications of one who does *ahiṃsā* are inexhaustible. Such a one is regarded as always performing sacrifices, and is the father and mother of all beings.
>
> *Mahābhārata* XIII:115:41

In these passages from the *Mahābhārata, ahiṃsā* is extolled as the best of all actions, giving birth to all righteousness or *dharma* and serving as the best possible means for purification. A chapter on *ahiṃsā* from the *Mahābhārata* will be discussed in chapter four.

In the classical Yoga system, which in a certain sense may be regarded as the premiere renouncer school of the Hindu tradition, wherein the values and some practices of the Jainas and Buddhists are given sanction within the framework of orthodoxy, *ahiṃsā* is mentioned as the basis of and the reason for all ethical practices. The commentator Vyāsa defines *ahiṃsā* as being the absence of injuriousness (*anabhidroha*) towards all living beings (*sarvabhūta*) in all respects (*sarvathā*) and for all times (*sarvadā*). It is said to result in the alleviation of enmity in the proximity of the one practicing *ahiṃsā* (*Yoga Sūtra* II:35). Vyāsa acknowledges that circumstantial exigencies might preclude the total practice of *ahiṃsā.* He gives as examples several cases in which one may be exempted from the practice of *ahiṃsā.* The first is that of the fisherman who only injures fish for his own survival. The second is the vow to abstain from killing only in a special place. Another case is the observation of harmlessness exclusively on particular days. In another hypothetical situation, an act of violence could be approved because it is committed for the gods or for a Brahman. Or, like a fisherman, a warrior can justify violence as being necessitated by his profession. In the final analysis, however, Patañjali, the author of the *Yoga Sūtra*, requires that the yogi practice *ahiṃsā* in its broadest sense (*mahāvratam*), unrestricted by caste (*jati*), place (*deśa*), time (*kāla*), or circumstance (*samaya*). *Ahiṃsā* here is required as the foremost spiritual discipline, to be strictly adhered to by aspiring yogis.

It is quite possible that Jaina attitudes from the sixth century B.C.E. had a direct influence on the development of the Yoga School; the first sequence of disciplines mentioned by Patañjali (circa 100 C.E.) are identical to the five vows of Mahāvīra's Jainism; nonviolence (*ahiṃsā*), truthfulness (*satya*), not stealing (*asteya*), sexual restraint (*brahmacharya*), and nonpossession (*aparigraha*). Due to the early date of Pārśvanatha (ca. 850 B.C.E.), it is also clear that Jainism is an earlier strata of the renouncer tradition that gave rise to both Yoga and Buddhism.

Throughout Indian history, there is evidence of the influence of *ahiṃsā* on political policy. This includes the rule of Aśoka during the third century B.C.E., which will be discussed in detail in the next chapter, and the Jaina kingships of Karnataka, which flourished from the second century until the thirteenth century of the common era.[47] Perhaps the most thoroughly documented instance of a non-Jaina ruler in India who was convinced to adopt nonviolence as a governmental policy occurred at the court of Akbar, the Moghul Emperor who extended Muslim control throughout most of India, ruling between 1556 and 1605. In 1582, Akbar invited the Jaina monk Hīravijaya Suri to visit the capital at Fatehpur Sikri in order to learn from him the basic principles of Jainism. The monk arrived in 1583 with an additional sixty-seven monks and stayed on for two years, giving private instruction to the Moghul ruler. Impressed with the "character and personality, learning and saintliness"[48] of the monk, Akbar gave him the title of Jagat-Guru or World Teacher, and asked how he could repay him for the teachings that had been given. Hīravijaya asked that Akbar use his influence to spread the teaching of nonviolence throughout the empire. In response, many prisoners were released and animal slaughter was prohibited every year during Jaina festival days in regions where Jainas lived.[49] Personally, Akbar was influenced by the Jaina philosophy of *ahiṃsā* and very nearly gave up eating meat and hunting. According to the *Akbar Nama*, he passed laws requiring the protection of mice, oxen, leopards, hares, fish, serpents, horses, sheep, monkeys, roosters, dogs, and hogs, either banning or limiting their slaughter.[50] Jaina influence was also seen in other voluntary legislation, such as the suggestion that *ahiṃsā* be practiced in the first month of the lunar cycle and that the use of leather be avoided in the sixth month. He also enacted legislation that hills sacred to Jainas be handed over to them in Gujarat and Bengal. Clearly, Akbar did much to advance the practice of *ahiṃsā* in India.

Conclusion

Nonviolence lies at the root of select forms of spiritual practice in the religious traditions of India, as we have seen in our brief survey. Regardless of religious distinctions, nonviolent action requires that the performer of any activity be aware of all of its implications. The concept of nonviolent action also presumes that another person is, in a fundamental sense, not different from oneself. Philosophically, non-difference of self and others provides a theoretical basis for performing nonviolence. Within the context of the Indian quest for liberation, nonviolence provides an important step toward the direct perception of the sacredness of all life. It serves to free one from restricted notions of self and to open one more fully to an awareness of and sensitivity toward the wants and needs of other persons, animals, and the world of the elements, all of which exist in reciprocal dependence.

For the Buddhists and Jainas, there is no creator god, only a continuation of what has been: time is beginningless, as is life itself. Each life state is interrelated and interchangeable, constantly taking new birth after the death of each particular form. The human condition is the highest, most desireable form of life, but is viewed in context as relating to and dependent upon virtually all other life forms. According to the *Chāndogya Upaniṣad*, the elements of the body, when cremated, enter into the atmosphere, join with the rain, return to earth, enter the plants, are consumed by humans, and form the seeds for new life. There is a continuity of substance between one's old body and a future embodiment. According to some schools of thought, after one dies the impressions of the life that has passed continue and find a new embodiment. Depending upon the nature of these impressions (*saṃskāras*), one can achieve a higher birth or a lower birth. Hence, the life force of an animal can evolve into human status; the opposite can also take place.

Given that all life forms are part of the same continuum, the consequences of one's actions require great consideration. This chapter began with a discussion of the importance of karma in Indian religions. The law of karma states that as you have done to others, so will be done to you, succinctly expressed by the Buddha at the beginning of the *Dhammapada*:

> If a man speaks or acts with an evil thought, evils follow him even as the wheel follows the foot of the ox which draws the cart.
>
> If a man speaks or acts with a pure thought, happiness follows him like a shadow that never leaves him.[51]

Action (karma) in the present will make its presence felt at a later time. Through accumulation of merits, one can avoid painful experiences in the future. The most obvious painful act is one of violence; by abstaining from violent acts, one can avoid incurring a karmic deposit which will require retribution in the future. This cornerstone of renouncer thought, so eloquently and simply expressed by the Buddha, and in many ways so uniquely Indian, migrated from India into East Asia not through the Jainas, who have traditionally considered farflung travel as productive of too much violence, but with the Buddhist renouncers who sailed and wandered into China and then Japan.

Chapter 2

Nonviolence, Buddhism, and Animal Protection

The Jaina tradition, with its biologically suffused cosmology, sophisticated psychology of karma, and intricate array of nonviolent lifestyles, provides an unparalleled paradigm for the practice of nonviolence. Though sometimes dismissed as extremist, the Jaina world view is noteworthy for its internal consistency and its constancy over millenia. Though it has spawned various subsects, it has not undergone any major doctrinal revisions since its first known articulation in the *Ācārāṅga Sūtra.*

Buddhism shares much in common with Jainism. Its founder, Gautama Buddha, lived from 563 to 483 B.C.E. and is said by some to have been a contemporary of Mahāvīra, the founder of Jainism. Buddhism, like Jainism, originated in India as a religious movement easily distinguishable from Hinduism due to its lack of allegiance to Vedic texts and its disdain for animal sacrifice. Both have been identified within India as Śramaṇa or renouncer traditions. Both emphasize monasticism. Like Jainism, Buddhism does not allow for a creator god; the cycle of life has been present from beginningless time. Unlike Jainism, Buddhism does not posit an abiding life force (*jīva*) but asserts that all phenomena are without lasting self-nature. Two other major features distinguish Buddhism from Jainism: it developed several distinct schools of thought and practice, and it traveled far from its native India, reaching virtually all parts of Asia.

Both Jainism and Buddhism hold fundamental the precept of not taking life. Though for the most part Buddhists do not maintain prohibitions against harming plants, and certainly do not consider the earth and water to be living, most schools of Buddhism uphold the notion that animal life must be protected,[1] though the degree to which this is enacted varies widely from country to country. In the previous chapter, mention has been made of the status and treatment of animals in the Jaina tradition. In this chapter we will investigate the appropriation of the nonviolent ethic by the early Buddhist community, particularly as expressed in stories regarding animals. We will then examine various Mahāyāna sources for the treatment of animals, many of which emphasize the teachings of universal compassion so prevalent in that tradition. Folk tales and poems about animals from Chinese and Japanese Buddhism will also be surveyed, providing delightfully graphic embellishments. At the conclusion of this chapter we will attempt to see how attitudes toward animals found in Jainism and Buddhism might be interpreted in light of the contemporary animal rights movement.

Respect for Animals in Early Buddhism

The treatment of animals is included in the first Buddhist precept—not to harm or injure living things (*prāṇātipātādviratiḥ*). In the *Mahāvagga*, the Buddha proclaims: "A *bikkhu* [monk] who has received ordination ought not intentionally to destroy the life of any living being down to a worm or an ant."[2] This concern for animal and plant welfare shaped monastic life. In the early days of the Buddhist community, the monks traveled during all three seasons, winter, summer, and the rainy season. The public, however, protested that "they crush the green herbs, they hurt vegetable life, they destroy the life of many small living beings," particularly when traveling during the rainy season.[3] Subsequently, the Buddha required that all the monks enter retreats and stop wandering during the monsoons. This public protest clearly indicates that the practice of *ahiṃsā* had by that time exerted broad influence, sufficient for people to advocate the adoption of this ethic by members of a religious order.

One indicator of the Buddhist commitment to the ethic of not injuring life forms is found in the abundant references to animals in the teachings of both the Buddha and the later Buddhists. For instance, in the *Jātakamālā*, didactic tales told by the Buddha drawn from his past lives, he portrays himself as a rabbit, a swan, a fish, a quail, an ape, a woodpecker, an elephant, and a deer. Animals are said to have contributed to his desire for *nirvāṇa*; seeing animals and humans suffer caused Buddha to seek enlightenment. In one such story, the future Buddha nurses back to health a goose that had been shot by his cousin Devadatta. In another anecdote, he feels compassion when he sees a tired farmer plowing the earth, a bird eating a worm dredged up by the plow, and the welts inflicted on the back of the ox by the farmer; the weariness of both beast and man helped initiate his quest for total awakening.

In the Buddhist tradition, the teaching of rebirth states that humans can be reborn as animals if they commit heinous deeds, and that animals can be reborn as humans if they exert effort to act meritoriously. As James P. McDermott has written:

> After the breaking up of the body after death, individuals of comparatively good conduct will be reborn in a relatively satisfactory state of existence (*sugati*), such as the human state. Those of bad conduct and wrong views, to the contrary, are destined to attain a miserable rebirth (*duggati*) as an animal or worse. Thus, for example, if they do not end up in hell itself, individuals who creep or slink along in this life, be they bloody-handed hunters, robbers, or whatever, are most likely to be reborn in the form of a sneaky or creeping creature—as a "snake, a scorpion, a centipede, a mongoose, a cat, a mouse, an owl" or the like.[4]

In the early texts, great care is taken not to harm animals for fear that other members of the offended species might take retribution,[5] or that one might be reborn as that same sort of animal.

Animals are depicted as being capable of meritorious behavior. In one passage from the *Vinaya Piṭaka*, an instance of amity among a partridge, a monkey, and an elephant is cited as exemplary for Buddhist monks.[6] In the *Nigrodhamiga-Jātaka*, a prior incarnation of the Buddha in the form of a deer offers his own life to replace that of a pregnant doe headed for slaughter. The deer's generosity appealed to the reigning king's sense of compassion, who then granted "guarantees for the protection of all deer in the park, and ultimately for all animals, birds, and fish in the realm."[7]

Animals are also deemed receptive to hearing and learning the teachings of the Buddha. In one instance, the Buddha approached a wild buffalo who had been causing trouble on the outskirts of a small village. He preached to him about "impermanence, lack of substance, and peaceful *nirvāṇa*. He also reminded him of his past births....Overcome with remorse, the buffalo died and was reborn in the Devaloka,"[8] the realm of the gods. In another story the Buddha pacified a greedy cobra and chastized him for his behavior, warning that his action would cause rebirth in hell. The snake reportedly "died thinking of the Buddha and was reborn in one of the heavens."[9]

In some instances in Buddhist literature, animals are portrayed as sacrificing their lives for the sake of human beings. In other cases, humans are seen as giving up their own flesh and sometimes their lives so that animals may survive. The *Avadāna-kalpalatā* tells of an elephant who throws himself off a rock in the desert to rescue starving travelers. A lion and an elephant rescue some men from a dragon, sacrificing their lives in the process.[10] In the *Śaśa Jātaka*, a rabbit offers his body to a Brahman for food, jumping into fire piled up by the rabbit himself. The Brahman was in fact the god Indra in disguise, who then placed the figure of the rabbit in the moon.[11] But these stories are only half the picture. Several parables and birth stories tell of humans sacrificing their flesh so that animals may keep living. In the *Jātaka Mālā*, the *Suvarṇaprabhāṣa*, and the *Avadāna-kalpalatā*, a story is told in which a Buddhist throws himself before a hungry tigress so that she may feed her cubs.[12]

One *Jātaka* tale is particularly instructive in regard to the importance of noninjury to living beings:

> Once upon a time, a goat was led to a temple and was about to be sacrificed by the presiding Brahman. Suddenly, the goat let out a laugh and then uttered a moaning cry. The Brahman, startled by his odd behavior, asked the goat what was happening. The goat responded as follows: "Sir, I have just remembered the history of what has led up to this event. The reason I have laughed is that I realized that in the last of 500 births I have suffered as a goat; in my next life I will return again as a human. The reason I have cried is out of compassion for you. You see, 500 births ago I was a Brahman, leading a goat to the sacrifice. After killing the goat, I was condemned to 500 births as a goat. If you kill me, you will suffer the same fate." The Brahman, visibly shaken, immediately freed the goat, who trotted away. A few minutes later, lightning stuck the goat and he was freed to again become human. The Brahman likewise was spared, due to the goat's compassionate intervention.[13]

This story includes multiple facets of Buddhist teachings, including karma, rebirth, noninjury, and compassion. Its graphic indictment of animal sacrifice holds particular importance for this volume.

Government Protection of Animals in Buddhist India

The concern for animal welfare was not confined to the Buddhist monastic community. Aśoka, one of the best known Indian emperors (ca. 274–232 B.C.E.), converted to Buddhism and established several laws that required kind treatment to animals. These included restricting meat consumption, curtailing hunting, and establishing hospitals and roadside watering stations for animals. Excerpts from Aśoka's inscriptions are as follows, translated from rocks and pillars still standing throughout India:

> Formerly, in the kitchen of the Beloved of the gods, King Priyadarśin (Emperor Aśoka), many hundred thousands of animals were killed every day for the sake of curry. But now when this Dharma-rescript is written, only three animals are being killed (every day) for the sake of curry (viz.) two peacocks (and) one deer (and) the deer again, not always. Even these three animals shall not be killed in the future.[14]
>
> Everywhere in the dominion of the Beloved of the gods, King Priyadarśin (Emperor Aśoka)...everywhere (provision) has been made by the Beloved of the gods, King Priyadarśin, (for) two (kinds of) medical treatment (viz.) medical treatment for men and medical treatment for animals.
>
> And wherever there are no (medicinal) herbs that are suitable for men and suitable for animals, everywhere (such) have been caused to be brought and caused to be planted.
>
> And whenever there are no (medicinal) roots and fruits, everywhere (such) have been caused to be brought and caused to be planted.
>
> And on the road, wells have been caused to be dug and trees have been caused to be planted, for the use of animals and men.[15]
>
> On bipeds and quadrupeds, on birds and aquatic animals, various benefits have been conferred by me (even) as far as the grant of life.[16]
>
> The Beloved of the gods, King Priyadarśin (Emperor Aśoka), spoke thus:
>
> (When I am) crowned twenty-six years, these various (animals) are declared by me inviolable, viz.—Parrots, mainas, the aruna, ruddy geese, wild ducks, the nandīmukha, the gelāṭa, bats, the ambākapīlikā, small tortoises, boneless fish, the vedaveyaka, the gaṅgā-puputaka, the sankuja fish, large tortoises and porcupines, squirrels, young deer, bulls, the okapiṇḍa, wild asses, white pigeons, village pigeons, (and) all quadrupeds which are neither useful nor edible.
>
> Those she-goats, ewes and sows (which) are either with young or are giving milk (to their young), are inviolable, and (so) also (are) those (of their) young ones which are less than six months old....

> Husks containing living beings (i. e. insects) are not to be burnt.
>
> Forest are not to be burnt, either uselessely or for killing animals.
>
> One animal is not to be fed with another animal...on every fast-day, fish are inviolable and are not to be sold...[on specific days] he-goats, rams, boars, and other animals that are usually castrated are not to be castrated...[and] the branding of horses and bullocks is not to be done.[17]

Though in many ways only a partial assertion of animal rights, these inscriptions nonetheless reveal a highly unusual compassion on the part of a temporal ruler towards his subjects, both human and natural.

It should be noted here that animal protection did not necessarily require vegetarianism on the part of the early Buddhists, nor is it observed universally by all Buddhist monks today. Though, as we will see, Buddhism in China clearly mandated a vegetarian diet, in Southeast Asia and in Tibet, a less stringent interpretation was given to the non-taking of life. In many instances, any food given to a monk is to be graciously accepted, as long as the food was not especially prepared. The act of giving on the part of the layperson serves to increase that person's merit. In a certain sense, the welfare of the recipient monk is secondary, both in terms of his or her sustenance and in terms of the violence indirectly committed. Giving (*dāna*) takes precedence over noninjury (*avihiṃsā*).[18] With the development of the Māhayāna school of Buddhism and the rise of compassion as the primary virtue, vegetarianism increased in popularity, to the extent that all Buddhist food in China is vegetarian.

Nonviolence toward Animals in East Asia

The geographical spread of ideas is one of the most intriguing and elusive concepts to pursue, regardless of discipline. As we have seen in the previous chapter, the *ahiṃsā* ethic, which perhaps had its origins in the Indus Valley civilization, finds a place in the religious literature of India starting about 600 B.C.E.; it was widely observed by Jainas, Buddhists, and select members of the Hindu community. The amalgamated Indian tradition that arose from this early period, primarily in its Buddhist and Hindu forms, spread through Asia and the Pacific region beginning approximately 100 B.C.E. Buddhist ideas and practices traveled via ship and overland into China, Southeast Asia and Indonesia; Hinduism likewise continues to assert its presence as far east as Bali. Victor H. Mair has attempted to show how the Indian tradition of picture recitation (telling stories with the assistance of large, transportable illustrations) traveled from its home in India to central Asia, Indonesia, China, the Middle East, and even Europe.[19] Citing Brahmanical, Jaina, and Buddhist precedents, he traces its spread during the seventh century into China as part of a number of cultural "transformations" that also include the entry of Manichaeanism.[20] In this next section, we will investigate how vegetarianism and animal protection, the most easily identifiable expressions of *ahiṃsā*, were received in East Asian cultures.

As noted by D. Seyfort Ruegg, the drive toward active animal compassion and vegetarianism was promoted especially by the Māhayāna school.[21] The *Laṅkāvatāra Sūtra*, one of the early texts of the Māhayāna school (and especially linked to Zen Buddhism), makes an eloquent appeal for vegetarianism and respect for animals in its eighth chapter.[22] Grounded in the theory of karma, the small excerpt below expresses the sentiment that prompted a concern for nonviolence in diet:

> In the long course of saṃsāra, there is not one among living beings with form who has not been mother, father, brother, sister, son, or daughter, or some other relative. Being connected with the process of taking birth, one is kin to all wild and domestic animals, birds, and beings born from the womb.[23]

The viewpoint that all life is interrelated was used to promote the abstention from meat, and within a Buddhist context serves as a basis for protesting all maltreatment of animals.

The *Laṅkāvatāra Sūtra* also includes stories to emphasize the need for vegetarianism. The text states that "even Indra who had obtained sovereignty over the gods had once to assume the form of a hawk owing to his habit-energy of eating meat for food in a previous existence."[24] It then tells of

> ...a king who was carried away by his horse into a forest. After wandering about in it, he committed evil deeds with a lioness out of fear for his life, and children were born to her. Because of their descending from the union with a lioness, the royal children were called the Spotted-Feet, etc. On account of their evil habit-energy in the past when their food had been flesh, they ate meat even [after becoming] kings, and...because they were excessively attached and devoted to meat-eating they gave birth to Dākās and Dākinīs who were terrible eaters of human flesh. In the life of transmigration...such ones will fall into the wombs of such excessive flesh-devouring creatures as the lion, tiger, panther, wolf,

> hyena, wild-cat, jackal, owl, etc.; they will fall into the wombs of still more greedily flesh-devouring and still more terrible Rākshasas. Falling into such, it will be with difficulty that they can ever obtain a human womb; how much more [difficult] attaining Nirvana![25]

These stories are of the genre of the fantastic Chinese tale, several examples of which will be given below.

The eighth chapter of the *Laṅkāvatāra Sūtra* answers many objections to the requirement that all Buddhist monks be vegetarian. It states that those who teach that the Buddha allowed meat-eating or that he himself died from eating bad meat are wrong. The discourse includes the following assertion:

> [T]he food for my Śrāvakas, Pratyekabuddhas, and Bodhisattvas is the Dharma and not flesh food; how much more the Tathāgata! The Tathāgata is the Dharmakāya, Mahāmati; he abides in the Dharma as food; his is not a body feeding on flesh; he does not abide in any flesh food. He has ejected the habit-energy of thirst and desire which sustain all existence; he keeps away the habit-energy of all evil passions; he is thoroughly emancipated in mind and knowledge; he is the All-knower; he is All-seer; he regards all beings impartially as an only child; he is a great compassionate heart. Mahāmati, having the thought of an only child for all beings, how can I, such as I am, permit the Śrāvakas to eat the flesh of their own child? How much less my eating it! That I have permitted the Śrāvakas as well as myself to partake of [meat-eating], Mahāmati, has no foundation whatever.[26]

This chapter ends with twenty-four verses advocating vegetarianism, the essence of which is communicated in the following:

> 2. Meat is not agreeable to the wise; it has a nauseating odour, it causes a bad reputation, it is food for the carnivorous; I say this Mahāmati: it is not to be eaten.[27]
>
> 14. [The meat-eater] is ill-smelling, contemptuous, and born deprived of intelligence; he will be born again and again among the families of the Caṇḍāla, the Pukkasa, and the Domba.[28]
>
> 23. [Meat-eating] is forbidden by me everywhere and all the time for those who are abiding in compassion; [he who eats meat] will be born in the same place as the lion, tiger, wolf, etc.

> 24. Therefore, do not eat meat which will cause terror among people, because it hinders the truth of emancipation; [not to eat meat—] this is the mark of the wise.[29]

This chapter contains perhaps the strongest advocacy of vegetarianism in the Buddhist tradition, and helped shape strict adherence to this practice in the Chinese monastic tradition.

The *Daśabhūmika Sūtra,* another important Māhayāna text, states that a Buddhist "must not hate any being and cannot kill a living creature even in thought."[30] Kṣemendra writes, "I cannot endure the pain even of an ant."[31] In the *Bodhisattva-bhūmi* discussion of giving (*dāna*), the first of the six perfections (*pāramitā*), the Buddhist is not allowed to give anything that "may be used to inflict injury on other living beings," nor is one allowed to give "poisons, weapons, intoxicating liquors, and nets for the capture of animals." A Buddhist must "not bestow upon others a piece of land on which the animals may be hunted or killed."[32]

The sixteenth minor precept in the *Fan-wang-ching (Brahmajāla Sūtra),* a text popular in China, graphically states that "One should be willing to forsake one's entire body, one's flesh, hands, and feet as an offering to starving tigers, wolves, lions, and hungry ghosts."[33] Although this example is undoubtedly overstated, the message is clear that animals are to be treated with great respect.

Government Protection of Animals in East Asia

The policy of animal protection that had first been declared by the Indian emperor Aśoka spread with Buddhism to China and Japan, where it periodically gained favor as a means of earning merit. The twentieth precept of the *Fan-wang-ching* (*Brahmajāla Sūtra*) declares:

> If one is a son of Buddha, one must, with a merciful heart, intentionally practice the work of liberating living beings. All men are our fathers, all women are our mothers. All our existences have taken birth from them.
>
> Therefore all living beings of the six *gati* [animals, humans, gods, titans, demons, hungry ghosts] are our parents, and if we kill them, we will kill our parents and also our former bodies, and all fire and wind are our original substance.
>
> Therefore you must always practice liberation of living beings *[hojo]* (since to produce and receive life is the eternal law) and cause others to do so; and if one sees a worldly person kill animals,

> he must by proper means save and protect them and free them from their misery and danger.[34]

The influence of this and other texts such as the *Suvarṇaprabhāṣa Sūtra* caused Chinese and Japanese leaders to declare the institution of *hōjō-e* or "meeting for liberating living beings." In the sixth century, the monk Chi-i reportedly convinced more than 1000 fishermen to give up their work. He also purchased 300 miles of land as a protected area where animals could be released. In 759 C.E. the Chinese Emperor Suh-tsung established 81 ponds where fish could be released; this was followed by similar actions on the part of Emperor Chen-Tsung (1017 C.E.).

George Clarke, a nineteenth-century missionary and observer of Chinese culture, has described the process of setting animals free as follows:

> In many parts of China the virtuous people have what is called a Fang Sen Hwie, i.e. a "Society for Liberating Life." It is believed that animals, birds, fishes and insects are possessed by someone's spirit; if their death is prevented the spirit obtains some mitigation of the pains of hell: therefore much merit is obtained by setting at liberty living creatures. A meeting of the members is convened every year. If near the water, as at Ta-li Fu, they have a picnic on the water, fishermen do a good trade by selling live fish cheaply, and their purchasers throw them into the lake. Sometimes sparrows are bought, but I have never heard of an ox or a horse being bought for this purpose. First, it would be too dear, and, secondly, it would soon be re-captured.[35]

Confirmation of this practice was found by Clarke in the *Yü-Li* (*Precious Records*), a collection of stories he translated and published over a century ago. In one instance, a Buddhist priest told a young man to practice the release of animals, predicting that he would then excel in higher education. Eventually, the lad became Chancellor of the Exchequer.[36]

In Japan, this movement was sponsored by Emperor Temmu Tennō, who restricted the use of certain hunting devices and the eating of cow, horse, dog, and monkey meat in 675 C.E.; he then ordered that various provinces "let loose living things" the following year. In 741 the Emperor Shōmu Tennō ordered prohibition against hunting and fishing on the fast days of the month. His daughter, the Empress Kōken, issued several similar decrees.[37] The release of living beings continues to be practiced in the East Asian world, primarily as a ceremonial event,[38] and has also been practiced by Buddhists in North America.[39]

Confucian Resistance to Vegetarianism

Vegetarianism as introduced by the Buddhists from India imprinted Chinese culture with the mark of nonviolence. As noted by Michael Freeman, by the time of the Sung Dynasty (960–1279 C.E.), "Buddhism...played a role in eveyone's life," with Buddhist dietary practices, including vegetarianism, gaining ascendancy over those of the Taoists.[40] This tradition still can be found in the modern Chinese restaurant, where vegetarian items are generally entitled "Buddhist Delight."

Perhaps more telling is the evidence of Buddhism's cultural impact that can be found in the negative reaction it prompted on the part of Confucian thinkers. Whereas Indian picture recitation easily could be assimilated and used for the expression of Chinese cultural sensibilities, the nonviolent ethic preached by the Buddhists threatened the very core of Confucian sensibility. As Kenneth Ch'en has noted:

> The Confucian viewpoint was that a heavenly decree controlled the fates of kingdoms and men, and there was little that man could do about it. In response to Hui-yüan's teaching that one who killed living creatures must be punished by being reborn in hell, Huan Hsüan (369–404 C.E.) posed the question: If the material body composed of the four great elements of earth, fire, water, and air were not merely a dwelling place of the soul, and if the soul were not injured when the material body was destroyed, why then should be this heavy punishment of falling into hell for killing a living creature?[41]

Clearly, the very doctrine of karma upon which nonviolence is predicated came into direct conflict with the Chinese cosmological view that heaven and earth are the parents of all things; in Chinese thought, the person functions to balance these two forces yet is always in a sense subservient to them. During the Chin period (265–420 C.E.), Tai An-kung writes that "Wisdom and foolishness, good and evil, longevity or early death, failure or success, all have their predestined fate, and are not brought about by the accumulation of good or bad karma. Since heaven and earth are so profound, and *yin-yang* is so vast, would not a man living within their spheres be merely like a grain of rice in a great granary, or the tip of a fine hair on a horse's body?"[42] Tai An-kung further states that no human effort can undo the nature one is given at birth and that misfortune happens even to the virtuous.

One item in particular is routinely criticized: the Buddhist dedication to nonviolence. Ho Ch'êng t'ien (370-447 C.E.) writes:

> The domestic goose as a fowl swims on a clear pond, eating the young grass and not touching the living creatures that wriggle about. But it is taken by the cook and rarely can it avoid being killed and served on a dish. The swallow hovers leisurely above, seeking food, and is satisfied only with flying insects, but men all love it and are not afraid of it even when it makes its nest in the dwelling place. Now this is the case not only with the goose and the swallow, but also with all living creatures. From this we know that the one which kills living creatures does not reap an evil retribution, and the meritorious one receives no good reward. Therefore what is taught people is one thing, what is manifested in the work is another. I am very doubtful of this (the doctrine of karma).[43]

At times the attacks against Buddhism became quite vitriolic, with Hsün Chi, who was executed for attempted assassination in 547, writing:

> Now monks and nuns sit idly in meditation during the summer and do not even kill ants, [saying that they] value the lives of all beings. On the one hand, they scorn their rulers and parents, yet on the other they mistakenly are benevolent toward insects.... Sakyamuni teaches the prince not to act as a prince, the minister not to behave as a minister, and down to [the last], the son not to act as a son. The relationships are thus reduced to a state of confusion.[44]

Buddhist sensibilities threatened the Confucian world view and came to be associated with the downfall of dynasties, the destruction of family values, and the diminishment of economic welfare, due to its advocacy of renunciation and meditation.

Objections to Buddhist vegetarianism continued with the writings of Han Yü (768-824 C.E.). In a sparse biographical critique of Emperor Wu, he writes:

> There was only the Emperor Wu of the Liang who was on the throne for forty-eight years. First and last, he thrice abandoned the world and dedicated himself to the service of the Buddha. He refused to use animals in the sacrifices in his own ancestral temple. His single meal a day was limited to fruits and vegetables. In the end he was driven out and died of hunger. His dynasty likewise came to an untimely end. In serving the Buddha he was seeking good fortune, but the disaster that overtook him was only the

> greater. Viewed in light of this, it is obvious that the Buddha is not worth serving.[45]

William LaFleur has noted that for Han Yü, the "definition of man was in jeopardy. And since man makes and maintains himself by his definitions, his act of drawing boundaries, his *li*, it was man himself which was threatened."[46] LaFleur elsewhere has written that

> the Confucianists had always held that the human species, capable of learning to read and write, for instance, was vastly superior to all other kinds. While they appreciated animals and plants, they drew a very strict line between what was human and what was not. Consequently, they thought people ought to have no qualms about eating anything not human.[47]

The very notions of reincarnation ran counter to the most basic of Chinese sensibilities. Even Mo-zi, renowned for his doctrine of compassion regardless of familial relations, does not extend his universal love to nonhumans.

Further evidence of lingering distrust of Buddhist values is found during the Ming Dynasty, when the Jesuit Mateo Ricci, in his quest to convert the Confucian elite to Christianity, "poured ridicule upon the belief in transmigration as the fruit of one's actions and upon the prohibition against killing living creatures."[48]

Chinese Folk Tradition Accounts of Respect for Animal Life

Nonetheless, a Buddhist-inspired enthusiasm for animals is found in a variety of contexts in Chinese and Japanese culture. In a wonderful story translated by Donald E. Gjertson, a peasant called Chih-tsung, who lived during the Sung dynasty, fell into a sort of coma for an extended period of time. When he finally revived, he told of being bound up and taken away by one hundred men who took him to a Buddhist shrine. In a decidely shamanistic fashion, he was seized by a monk who stated:

> "You are fond of hunting and fishing and ought now to receive retribution."
>
> He then took Chih-tsung, peeled off his skin, and pared away his flesh the way one would go about dressing down an animal. Next he was placed deep down under water, and then pulled out by hook in the mouth, to be split in two and chopped up into a

> fine hash, boiled in a caldron, and roasted over a brazier. Reduced to a pulp, he was made whole again and the process repeated with great pain and suffering. After a third time the monk stopped and asked whether or not he would like to live. Chih-tsung then bowed his head to the ground and pleaded for his life....
>
> Seeing several ants, the priest pointed to them and said, "Even though these are very insignificant beings, still they must not be killed. How much the less those that are larger!"
>
> ...Chih-tsung then returned to life and after several days was able to get up. Thereafter he ceased his hunting and fishing.[49]

According to this Chinese Buddhist story, dire punishments are in store for persons who eat meat.

Similarly, those who do evil deeds are destined to be reborn as an animal in their next life. Chao T'ai, a bureaucrat within the Chin dynasty (265-420 C.E.) is said to have collapsed, was pronounced dead, and then later revived. After his recovery, he told of what he experienced in the land of the dead. Along with several thousand men and women, he appeared before a magistrate, to whom he proclaimed he had not committed any evil. Consequently, he was appointed as Inspector of Waterworks and later promoted to Supervisor, which entitled him to oversee various soldiers. Their mission was to inspect the various hells to which sinners had been sent. Harsh punishments abounded: some were poked through with needles, some were being boiled in large caldrons, others were impaling themselves on trees made from swords, severing their own bodies and heads. Beyond this was the City of Transformation, where those who had accepted Buddhist teaching could receive a new birth assignment in accord with their past karma. Within this area,

> there were several hundred bureau officials who were examining and collating documents, saying that those who had engaged in killing were to become mayflies which are born in the morning and die in the evening; those who engaged in stealing and robbery were to become pigs and sheep, to be butchered and cut up by others; those who engaged in sexual wantonness were to become cranes, ducks, and deer; the double-tongued were to become owls; those who did not repay their debts were to become donkeys, mules, oxen, and horses.

Following this extensive moral lesson, Chao T'ai was sent back to earthly life and exhorted his relatives to "mend their ways and honor the Dharma, and enjoined them to strive energetically after the good."[50]

In a similar tale said to have occurred in 758 during the T'ang dynasty, a Keeper of Records called Hsueh Wei lost consciousness for twenty days. When he miraculously revived, his first words urged his family to see if his fellow officials were eating minced fish. Although puzzled by this strange request, a servant was sent and confirmed that Officials of the Judiciary Department were eating a large carp. Amazed at their friend's recovery and intrigued by his telepathy, they went to his bedside where he told them all the details regarding the procurement of the magnificent specimen they had been consuming. When they asked, "But how did you know all of this?" he replied, "The carp you killed was I!" He then went on to relate that when he lost consciousness he found himself at the banks of the river. Due to the uncomfortable heat, he pulled off his clothes and jumped in, instantly transforming into a magnificent carp. A fish-headed man then told him that he longed for "complete freedom and leisure," but that he must be wary of the fisherman's hook. Eventually, due to hunger, Hsueh Wei succumbed to temptation and was caught. His protests went unheeded first to his captor, then to the various persons who marvelled at the size of the carp, and then finally to the cook:

> "I said to all of you, 'I am your colleague, and may be killed today. Ignoring my pleas, you do not let me go, but rush me off to my execution. Where is your humanity?'
>
> "I shouted and wept, but you didn't even turn a hair. You just handed me over to the mincemeat maker. Cook Wang, who was just sharpening a knife, was happy to see me and tossed me onto the table.
>
> "Again I cried out, 'Cook Wang! You've been my mincemeat maker for a long time. How can you kill me? Why don't you attend to my words and relate them to the other officials?'
>
> "But Cook Wang didn't seem to hear. He held my neck firmly on the chopping board, and lopped off my head. As my head fell, I came back to my senses. And then I called you all here."
>
> Every one of the officials was amazed. They were awakened to a new sense of pity for all living things. For every one of them...had seen the fish's mouth move, but had not heard a thing.
>
> From then on Wei's three friends gave up minced fish, and never ate it again as long as they lived.[51]

In a variation on this theme, another tale tells of a man called Yü I-lang who "took ill in the year 1192 and was dragged into the wild by two ghost guards." He then confronted the ten kings of the various hells, who questioned Yü about his past activities and "decided to add two years to his life in recognition of the many times he had saved the lives of animals." Yü's life was then restored, to "live out his extended lifespan."[52]

Stern warnings are given in the Yü-Li regarding the fate of those who take the lives of animals:

> Those who kill the ox (which ploughs the field) or the dog (who watches the house), or animal life in general, their souls shall be placed before the mirror of reflection. After suffering the torments of the...hells,...a red-haired, black-faced demon shall cut such from the head to the buttocks. The suffering is intense. After healing, they shall be cast for ten years into a great hell, then in the scalding water hell for fifteen years. They shall appear before the judge, who shall condemn them to receive 1,500 calamities in the boundless hell. At the expiration of this ordeal they shall be sent to the wheel of life and be born again as beasts.[53]

If, by chance, such a person has not eaten beef or dog flesh, he or she would be spared the hell experience; if they have, through their "exhortation caused one hundred persons to refrain from eating beef or dog's flesh, and have given away thirty good books, they shall be born again in the happy land."[54]

Vegetarianism and noninjury to animals weighs heavily in the nature of one's path after death. Numerous stories are told about persons who have abstained from consuming animal flesh with wondrous results, as opposed to meateaters who suffer certain misfortune. In one, a mother laments because she is certain that the cries of pig being slaughtered are in fact the cries of her own daughter who was reborn as a swine due to her gluttonous consumption of fowl (700 per year) before her untimely death at the age of seventeen.[55] In another, a man called Shiao dreamed that a god told him that if he became vegetarian he would live until the age of eighty; the man did so, became a scholar, and died without illness at the age of ninety-five.[56]

Although these many stories clearly emerge from a folk milieu and come to form their own special genre of fantastic tales, the underlying world view is unmistakably consistent: persons and even animals are held accountable for their actions, even if the punishment or reward does not occur until after death. The following passage, which occurs at the end of Clarke's text after detailed descriptions of the various hells, summarizes this tradition of after-life retribution, borrowed from India but embraced in China with graphic zeal:

> Those who have been unfilial and wantonly destroyed life, having received full punishment in the previous hell, upon their arrival here, shall be changed from their original forms and when liber-

> ated into the world they shall be animals. Whatever animal, bird, fish or insect, that during its existence as such has not injured any creature, shall be advanced in its next transformation and by degrees attain to human existence.[57]

As Donald Gjertson has noted, this tradition first appears in China in the early fifth century C.E., apparently when Buddhism becomes thoroughly appropriated into Chinese culture and imaginative structures. He notes, however, that these stories are very much concerned with life in this world; virtually no mention is made of enlightenment. Rather, "the miracle tales seem to show that the principal thrust of popular Buddhist piety lay...in the amelioration of one's present human situation and the hope for future rebirth into a good mode of existence."[58] Given the initial and persistent resistance to Buddhism documented above, the story tradition attests to the absorption into the culture of Buddhist ideas such as are found in the *Laṅkāvatāra Sūtra*; respect for animal life came to permeate and transform folk behavior.

Poetic Expression of Respect for Animals in Chinese Tradition

In addition to the fear-of-hell and animal story traditions through which both the value and importance of respecting all forms of life are communicated, another genre also attests to the absorption of the *ahiṃsā* doctrine into Chinese culture. In 1928 a collection of illustrated Chinese poems entitled *Hue Shen Hua Chi* was complied, comprised of works by both Buddhist monks and lay people. Dr. Raghu Vira, who through the International Academy of Indian Culture in Nagpur, arranged for these to be translated into Sanskrit and English, wrote that these illustrated poems "catch the cruelty that is being perpetrated on the poor creatures, whether for food, fun or sport, wittingly or unwittingly, and to portray the same with the power and refinement of a gentle and magnanimous soul."[59] Raghu Vira asserts that such a document has no parallel in India, where, I might add, the poetic sense requires a more stylized and descriptive form. In the first poem cited below, the lowly pig is seen as not different from the human being, in that both experience physicality and emotional grief. Persons are urged to abstain from eating meat, on the basis that it extends one's "love of humanity," an ironically Confucian allusion:

Flesh of Our Flesh

The swine are also sentient beings.
Their bodies possess the same elements as ours.
Seeing their grievance and helplessness

Rouses the all-mighty heart of sympathy.
An appeal to the world of man—
For the sake of protecting life,
Do not kill.
And, when you do not eat flesh,
You have already done a job for the love of humanity.[60]

This poem invites a person to consider the life of pigs and to see them as not different from the human order. By loving animals, the author suggests, love is expressed for humanity itself.

In the following poem, the cooperative spirit of crabs is seen as providing an exemplar of compassion that humans should emulate. This scenario is similar in tone to some of the Jātaka tales mentioned earlier in which animals sacrifice themselves for the sake of others:

To the Rescue

One crab has lost its legs.
Two crabs come to its rescue,
And carry it on their sturdy sympathetic backs.
These tiny wee creatures have the sense
Of love and compassion.
Of this why does man not take notice?[61]

The work of contemporary biologist Donald Griffin has ascertained that animals experience feelings much the same as humans do.[62] This scientific breakthrough, clearly at odds with Descartes' statements that animals are mechanistic and unfeeling, as well as with the attitudes of many modern scientists, finds verification in the following verse:

Mummy's Feathers

They are Mummy's remaining feathers,
That young ones are mournfully watching.
They do not know that the mother is dead,
Yet they watch and watch and watch.
Look in this scene of parental love,
One can not but be moved to the utmost.[63]

Advocacy of vegetarianism is clearly reflected in the following two poems, which urge the reader to see the universality of the will to live and also to contemplate the defilement that can breed in flesh foods:

Kidnapped

Where there is life there is a desire to live,
Here there is no difference between man and beast.
The most frightful thing is to kill,
The most painful thing is to vivisect.
When a fowl is caught, though not killed,
It is already frightened to death.
When you cut its throat it tosses with agony.
And when one ponders over this,
How can one have the heart to eat flesh![64]

Exhumation

How can they be called delicious dishes?
They are merely rotten, stinking, unnatural and what not;
Tears well up in one's eyes,
Sick is one's heart,
When the scene is viewed.
The wise feels ashamed and downcast.[65]

These poems communicate a fervent commitment to the nonviolent ethic. As Raghu Vira has noted, "Neither the Buddhists, nor the Jainas, not the Vaishnavas have anything similar to offer. It was left to the Chinese genius to catch the cruelty that is being perpetrated on the poor creatures, whether for food, fun or sport, wittingly or unwittingly...."[66] This thoroughly indigenous aesthetic expression indicates the deep and pervasive impact that nonviolent values made upon some sectors within China.

Respect for Animals in Japanese Buddhist Tradition

With the transmission of Buddhism from China to Japan, the *ahiṃsā* doctrine underwent yet another cultural transformation. Perhaps the most significant change that was made is to be found in the Noh play tradition's proclamation that plants have Buddha-nature, which will be discussed in greater detail in the next chapter. As in China, stories were designed to encourage the protection of animals, and the protection of those releasing animals. William LaFleur has commented that, in general, the Japanese did not resist the notion of the sanctity of animal life as did the Confucians in China. The Shinto tradition in fact could be seen as very supportive of such a view.

However, he has also stated that they did not necessarily obey the precept: fish is an integral part of the Japanese diet and is consumed even by Buddhist priests.[67] Unlike the practice in Tibet, where it was declared that it was better to slay one large yak than several small fish, the Japanese have not been inclined to use big animals for food.

Special days called "vegetarian meetings" are traditionally observed in Japan during which one eats nothing after noon, and only vegetarian food before noon. These days, referred to as Upostha in Sanskrit and Sai-e in Japanese, are held on the eighth, fourteenth, fifteenth, twenty-third, twenty-ninth, and thirtieth of each month. During portions of the months of January, May, and September, a similar fast is sometimes observed. The purpose of these is to accrue personal merit through the practice of virtue, and often they are offered for specific purposes such as good health and good fortune. The earliest mention of this practice is found in an edict of Emperor Bidatsu in 578; during the years 802–1467 it was celebrated each January 8–14 for the protection of the state, being one of three great festivals associated with the Nara period.[68]

Fantastic stories similar to those told in China were circulated in Japan to emphasize the importance and efficacy of practicing nonviolence to all life forms. In one such tale, a monk advises some people to buy four large sea turtles and then set them free. Later, the same monk is thrown overboard from a ship by thieving sailors and is presumed drowned. However, the four turtles that he had helped rescue come to his aid and deliver him to the beach, after nodding to him three times.[69] In a rather gruesome tale, a man is punished for abusing horses:

> In Kawachi province, there was once a man named Isowake who used to sell melons. He would saddle a horse with an overwhelming burden and, if it failed to move, would whip it angrily and drive it forward. The horse staggered along with its eyes full of tears. When Isowake had sold all of the melons, he would then kill the horse. After he had killed a number of horses in this way, Isowake happened to look into a kettle of boiling water, whereupon his two eyes fell into the kettle and were boiled.

The story ends with a statement regarding the karmic causality and the need to respect all animals:

> Swift is the penalty of evil deeds. How can we not believe in the law of karmic causality? Beasts in the present life might have been our parents in a past life. We pass through the six modes of exis-

> tence (gods, humans, demons, animals, hungry ghosts, and hell beings) and four manners of birth (from womb, egg, moisture, or heaven or hell). Reflection shows us that we cannot be without mercy.[70]

Unusual cruelty and immediate retribution are also demonstrated in another brief tale:

> In Yamato province there was a man whose name and native place are not identified. He was not benevolent and liked to kill living beings. He caught a rabbit and set it free in the fields after skinning it alive. Before long he contracted a fatal illness; his whole body was covered with scabs that broke out in extremely painful sores. He was never cured and died groaning loudly.
>
> Ah! How soon wicked deeds incur a penalty in this life! We should be considerate and benevolent. Above all, we should show mercy.[71]

In another story narrated by the monk Kyokai (who incidentally acknowledged that his genre of storytelling imitated similar Chinese texts), a wealthy householder, stricken with illness due to his sacrificial killing of one oxen per year for seven years, then dedicated himself to the practice of buying animals and setting them free. At the end of seven virtuous years he died, but then revived nine days later. He told his family that he had been judged in a subterranean court by seven oxen who prepared to chop him up and devour him. But then ten million men, who had been the creatures he had released, came to his rescue and restored him to earthly life.[72] In each of these tales, the graphic portrayal of violence against animals, and the equally grim retribution, serves a clearly didactic function, evincing a visceral reaction on the part of the one who hears or reads each episode.

In summary, Buddhism has developed an extensive tradition of emphasizing a link between the human realm and that of animals. Though Buddhism considers human birth superior, in that only humans can achieve *nirvāṇa*, various texts remind people that they once were animals and can again take animal birth if they behave incorrectly. Additionally, several stories tell of animals who perform virtuous actions and thus ensure for themselves either heavenly or human birth. Although the earliest forms of Buddhism did not advocate vegetarianism, monks were not allowed to accept meat dishes that had been cooked explicitly for them. This standard continues within the Theravāda school throughout Southeast Asia. In the Māhayāna tradition, which spread from northern India to East Asia, vegetarianism became a requirement, particularly for Chinese monks, causing a clash with indigenous Confucian culture, but securing a place deep within the folk tradition.

Animal Rights and Ahiṃsā

We have considered Jaina and Buddhist attitudes towards animals from a variety of textual sources and folk traditions. From the evidence surveyed, noninjury to animals clearly holds a prominent place in both traditions. Animals are regarded to be none other than our very selves. The underlying assumption is that each and every human being has experienced a wide variety of animal births in prior incarnations and that if one makes a mistake of significant proportions during human birth that one will again be born as an animal in punishment for wrongdoing. One of the great acts of wrongdoing that will cause rebirth as an animal is undue harm to an animal or human, both of which are to be seen as akin to oneself. By contrast, the status accorded to animals in most other cultures, especially those arising from Europe and America, regards animals to have no such kinship relationship. The book of Genesis and the writings of Aristotle, Augustine, Aquinas, Descartes, and others have justified the position that animals exist solely for human exploitation. Consequently, with the rise of science and technology, billions of animals are brought into the world each year by humans to be eaten as food and to be killed in laboratory experiments.[73] Additionally, wild animals are pushed from their native habitats by human development projects; millions of species not deemed useful have become extinct, and millions more species are threatened.

How might the nonviolent traditions of Jainism, Buddhism, and Yoga, all of which advocate the practice of *ahiṃsā*, react to this mass destruction? In regard to animal flesh being used as food, the answer is clear: Jainas, Yogis, and many Māhayāna Buddhists disdain the eating of meat. Members of these groups practice vegetarianism and have publicly advocated the banning of flesh foods for millenia. However, scientific research using animals is a uniquely modern phenomenon, as is the decimation of nonhuman species as a result of extraordinary human intervention. Obviously, no clear statement that could be applied to these problems can be found in the classical texts. One related issue that can be cited is that of animal sacrifice, performed by some Hindus and strongly condemned by both Buddhists and Jainas. The early Hindu community performed intricate rituals that culminated in the sacrifice of live animals. One such ritual, the horse sacrifice (*aśvamedha*), entailed releasing a horse for one year, following it as it wandered throughout India, and then killing and dismembering it. This ritual eventually became internalized and the process was visualized but not enacted.[74] For years, Buddhists and Jainas lobbied against all animal sacrifice, using the argument that such activities violated the first and most important ethical principle: nonviolence. They were successful in many respects. Within many later Hindu texts, nonviolence is accorded the same respect it is given in Jainism, as we have seen.[75] However, although the Jainas have successfully lobbied for the ban of this practice in most states in India, goat sacrifices continue to be practiced in Nepal[76] and the state of Orissa.

How might the classical Jaina and Buddhist position contribute to the current debate over the use and abuse of animals for scientific research? First, these traditions both view animals as sentient beings. Animals are said to have feelings and emotions and to be able to improve themselves, at least in some of the various parables that are cited. While Westerners may dismiss this as merely a naive anthropomorphism, it is instead a deeply rooted cultural perspective. In seeing animals as kin, that is, in accepting the theory of repeated birth in the form of increasingly or decreasingly sophisticated animals, depending upon one's deeds, the entire kingdom, humans included, becomes an extended family. For the Jainas, even rocks and streams are within the same continuum. By contrast, the one-life orientation of the prophetic religious traditions regards animals in an entirely differently light and has allowed for their sacrifice in the laboratory environment. For a Jaina or a Buddhist, this would be unthinkable. To kill is a great infraction against the religious precepts and certainly would result in future suffering.

The theory of karma as presented above is interpreted as a linear process; acts are committed by, and accrue to, one individual life. "If I do this good act now, I will earn merit which will be rewarded in the future" would be one expression of this reading, as would "the reason why I am so unfortunate now is because of evil acts I committed in the past." This mechanistic view unfortunately does not directly relate the effects of human action to society, though threats of karmic punishment are used to advocate socially responsible behavior. A modern reading of karma, which would dispose of the need for belief in reincarnation, and hence would be more accessible to the superstition-wary Westerner, would be to view it as horizontal instead of sequential. An action does not necessarily remain confined to one life, because its influence spreads out to the lives of others. If one acts violently and is imprisoned as a result, an entire family is affected. Similarly, actions by scientists affect society as a whole. This interpretation does not seek to dismiss the personal responsibility one carries but emphasizes the social dimensions of action. The rise of science has given birth to medicines and luxuries that have greatly eased human misery. But these same advances now plague the world with nuclear weaponry and chemical warfare, increased rates of cancer and heart diseases, and tragedies produced by such "improvements" as thalidomide and Agent Orange. It might be said that the violence that was involved in the development of these various substances is now being experienced indirectly as the widespread effects of these and other products of the technological age are being felt.

Both Buddhists and Jainas affirm the nobility of animals and humans who give their lives to others, as seen in the story of the elephant who spared the rabbit, and the story of the rabbit who jumped into the fire to feed a traveler. Such fantastic tales are designed to encourage humans to improve our own behavior. It might be possible to construe these anecdotes to legitimize the loss of animal life for the sake of science. But in each of the stories, the animals were not coerced into their acts of compassion but surrendered their lives out of their own will and desire. In the modern context, it is highly doubtful that any animal would march into a corporate research laboratory or volunteer to overdose on drugs or be injected with carcinogens.

It might be argued that medicines are needed to protect the human order, that we are waging a war against disease and we need to enlist the aid of animals in this just war. The Jainas, as we have seen, do in fact include within their system a provision for committing violence out of self-defense. An elder monk would not place himself in a situation that would require such an activity, but lay persons continually encounter a need for violence, however subtle, in order to survive. Would the threat of a disease, such as a plague that would undoubtedly kill thousands of people and could only be counteracted by medicines tested on animals, be an acceptable justification for restricted violence in "self-defense"? The response within the context of Jaina logic is not simple. The Jaina would not deny the validity of the argument for using animals in such research. According to their philosophies of *anekantavāda* (literally, "not only one solution") and *naya* (partial expression of truth), which will be considered in greater detail in chapter five, there is never a single valid perspective in a given situation: all truths are partial truths. The Jaina philosophy of nonabsolutism, an outgrowth of the *ahiṃsā* doctrine, would not allow a Jaina to hold an opinionated or rigid attitude about this or any other situation. Hence, a Jaina would probably not deny that the scientist who conducts such experiments has a legitimate viewpoint within the scientific milieu. Normally, the Jaina doctrines of karma and *ahiṃsā* would prohibit a Jaina from allowing the killing of animals to benefit himself or herself. Following the example of earlier Jainas, one might attempt to make the other side see the validity of the Jaina perspective and perhaps, at a minimum, convince them to declare days of abstinence from destruction, as was achieved through Jaina influence at Akbar's court.

In fact, the Jaina community controls much of the pharmaceutical industry in India and is undoutedly required to adhere to saftey and testing regulations. The compromise solution that the Jainas have put into practice combines modern exigency with tradition. Animals are used for testing but then are "rehabilitated" through shelters and recuperation facilities maintained by the laboratories. For instance, one Jaina-controlled pharmaceutical company uses animals for the production of immunoglobulin but then releases them into the wild.[77] This practice fits well with the ages-old Jaina tradition of constructing animal shelters for infirm animals, allowing them to survive until their natural demise.[78]

From a Buddhist perspective, the endeavors of experimental science might be regarded as useful in a limited way, being primarily concerned with manipulations on the level of *saṃsāra*. From the ultimate point of view, which is the prime concern of the Buddhist, such work would not ultimately prove worthwhile. Neither scientists nor disease victims nor animals have independent self-natures. All are composed of parts and are subject to decay and dissolution. All three need to be helped, not merely to live a longer or more comfortable life, but also to see their nonsubstantiality, their impermanence. For the Buddhist, avoidance of death, the telos of the scientific realm, would not be the highest value. Rather, the quality of death is most important, and this can only be determined by one's understanding of life. This is not to say that Buddhism looks forward to death; the earlier passages affirm the sanctity of life. We saw that Aśoka instituted the planting of medicinal herbs for both animals and humans. Medical and surgical cures are mentioned in the early Buddhist canon, and later Buddhism includes healing deities (Bhaiṣajya-rāja and Baiṣajya-samudgata) who assists in curative processes.[79] But when death becomes imminent it must be accepted, and the Buddhist must attempt to die freely, without attachment or fear.[80]

Putting these philosophical considerations aside, our problem remains: How might the Buddhist religion approach the modern practice of killing animals in research laboratories, given the long history of Buddhist kindness to all living things? Before passing judgment on any issue, Buddhism requires that three factors be taken into consideration: the intention of the act, the means used to execute it, and its consequences. This formula has been illustrated with a story told by the Buddha in which a ship with 500 people on board is threatened by an evil man who has the ability to kill all 500. The captain must decide whether to act against this man or not and, after having considered the intention and consequences of performing an act of violence, he kills the evil man, thus saving everyone else on board.[81] Could similar considerations be used by a contemporary Buddhist to agree to or to support the killing of animals in research laboratories? Three factors would have to be considered: intention, means, and consequences. The first category eliminates the bulk of possible circumstances: destruction of animals for instruction in high school biology classes would be deemed unnecessary, as would research conducted by cosmetic companies aimed at enhancing human vanity. Only in an extreme case would the intention be deemed acceptable, such as testing of a vaccine desperately needed to stave off an epidemic. Then the means would have to be considered. Can the pain be minimized? Are the animals well treated? Finally, the consequences have to be considered. Will lives in fact be saved? Will other reactions occur, such as genetic damage or increased risk of cancer on the part of the humans who use the product? Will the test merely lead to the proliferation of more tests, thereby endangering more lives, both animal and human?

The responses of modern Buddhist leaders and organizations in North America are quite clear in their position regarding animal welfare. Roshi Philip Kapleau, director of the Zen Center in Rochester, New York, has written several articles, as well as the book, *To Cherish All Life*, in defense of animals.[82] In California, students of the Tassajara Zen Monastery operated an organization, Buddhists Concerned for Animals, which lobbied for animal rights in farming, scientific experimentation, war research, and trapping. These movements, though small scale, have the potential to influence a larger population. Such efforts may appear insignificant, but must not be dismissed. The gentle persuasion of the Jainas, which has endured for centuries, has convinced major segments of the Indian population that the protection of living beings is both meritorious and desirable; similar efforts in the modern world might prove equally effective.

On the issue of single-species preservation, we again confront an issue that has no precendent in the era during which the classical texts were developed. In fact, some have suggested that the Endangered Species Act is a uniquely American phenomenon, emerging from a mindset that places ultimate value on individual freedom and liberty, in such a way that it extends to the nonhuman natural realm.[83] In a certain sense, this might seem at odds with Buddhist teachings that seek to overcome notions of ego identity: to ascribe essential nature to one particular sort of tree could seemingly lead to attachment for the tree. This attachment would then impede one from the attainment of *nirvāṇa* and thus be antithetical to the Buddhist endeavor. However, to the extent that one's own liberation entails cultivating a vision of Buddha nature that extends to all beings, affection and respect for life in all its myriad forms would be certainly part of the path to *nirvāṇa*. Furthermore, from the perspective of the Māhayāna school, which asserts that *saṃsāra* is none other than *nirvāṇa*, such an attitude would in fact be an enlightened attitude.

The Dalai Lama, exiled leader of the Tibetan people and an important contemporary world religious figure, has summarized the Tibetan Buddhist attitude toward life in the following passage, taken from a book published in 1980:

> In our approach to life, be it pragmatic or otherwise, a basic fact that confronts us squarely and unmistakably is the desire for peace, security, and happiness. Different forms of life at different levels of existence make up the teeming denizens of this earth of ours. And, no matter whether they belong to the higher groups such as human beings or to the lower groups such as animals, all beings primarily seek peace, comfort, and security. Life is dear to a mute creature as it is to man. Even the lowliest insect strives for protection against dangers that threaten its life. Just as each one of us want happiness and fear pain, just as each other one of us want to live and not to die, so do all other creatures.[84]

This approach to animals would certainly support efforts to preserve and maintain species that have come under assault, not out of sentimentality, but out of respect for their own needs and desires. The interconnectedness and interrelatedness of life would here serve as the essential rationale for protection of life. The preservation of individual identity is secondary. According to such texts as the *Laṅkāvatāra Sūtra*, we have all been related to one another at some time in the immeasurable history of living beings. The precepts of giving and noninjury to life urge persons to nurture life, giving to and protecting life, rather than abusing and using life for one's own gratification.

Chapter 3

Nonviolent Asian Responses to the Environmental Crisis: Select Contemporary Examples

In this chapter, Hindu, Jaina, and Buddhist responses to the environmental crisis will be examined in light of their respective integration of the nonviolent ethic. We will begin with a brief discussion of how the Vedic and Vedāntic philosophies of the Hindu religion have contributed a theoretical paradigm for the development of an ecological outlook, supplementing our earlier investigation of Jaina and Buddhist attitudes toward life. In the discussion that follows, we will begin with some anecdotes that show the ongoing concern for not hurting living beings in India. We will then examine Gandhian theory in light of its potential contribution to an ecological economics. This will be juxtaposed with some harsh realities from the industrialized, twentieth-century Indian landscape. Some contemporary environmental institutions and movements within India will then be discussed, including the Chipko movement. We then turn to a discussion of an ecologically sound lifestyle as modeled by the traditional wisdom of the Jaina religion. We will also look briefly at Buddhist attitudes toward nature that reflect an empathetic view, particularly as evidenced in the Noh play tradition and American Buddhist environmentalism. The chapter concludes with a reflective analysis of a possible interface between the newly emerging Gaian cosmology and traditional Jaina models of orthopraxy.

Possible Models for an Indigenous Indian Environmentalism

In the prior chapters, we suggested that the doctrine of nonviolence, with its attendant requirements of vegetarianism and reverence for animals, might have arisen from the Indus Valley civilization, which has been dated as early as five thousand years ago. The spread of the *ahiṃsā* doctrine into East Asia has been demonstrated in our examination of Buddhist practices and folk tales in East Asia. However, on the topic of environmental ethics, the Hindu tradition, which finds its primary authority in the Vedic literature, also offers conceptual resources that promote ecological sensitivity. In the Vedic hymns, we find an intimate relationship between persons and various personifications of the earth, water, thunderstorms, and so forth. The Vedic rituals, many of which are still performed today, invoke elemental forces. The Sāṃkhya tradition reveres the five great elements (*mahābhūta*) of earth, water, fire, air, and space as the essential building blocks of physical reality. From the Upaniṣads and later Vedāntic formulations, all things with form (*saguṇa*) are seen to be essentially nondifferent from the universal consciousness or ultimate reality; any thing with form can be an occasion to remember that which is beyond form (*nirguṇa*).

From the earliest strata of religion in South Asia we find evidence of a city culture attuned to and respectful of natural rhythms; the seals of the Indus Valley cities of Mohenjodaro and Harappa depict a meditating figure surrounded with lush vegetation and peaceful animals. The songs of the *Ṛg Veda* extol the powers and wonders of the earth, regarding them to be divinities worthy of worship. The rivers (Gāṅgā, Yamunā, Sarasvatī, Sindhu) and the earth (Pṛthivī) are regarded to be goddesses, while the winds (Maruts) and fire (Agni) are invoked as gods. From these hymns an image of the human person arose that sees a continuity between the individual and cosmos. The *Puruṣa Sūkta* states:

> The moon was born from his mind;
> His eyes gave birth to the sun;
> Indra and Agni came from his mouth;
> And Vāyu (the wind) from his breath was born.
> From his navel the midair rose;
> The sky arose from his head;
> From feet, the earth; from ears, the directions.
> Thus they formed the worlds.[1]

In this passage, an identity or correlation is proclaimed between the external world and the individual human person, indicating an intimate relationship between human beings and their environment. The unknown author likens thoughts to the moon, eyes to the sun, and the powers of victory and fire to the human mouth. The body finds its roots in the earth, stretching upward into the sky. In the Judeo-Christian story, God made men and women in his own image; in this primordial tale, which includes no creator god, the forces that compose the universe are also found within the human body.

This sense of continuity with nature is also found in the *Bṛhadāraṇyaka Upaniṣad*, which draws a simile between a tree and a person:

> As a tree of the forest,
> Just so, surely, is man.
> His hairs are leaves,
> His skin the outer bark.
> From his skin blood,
> Sap from the bark flows forth.
> From him when pierced comes forth
> A stream, as from the tree when struck.
> His pieces of flesh are under-layers of wood.
> The fiber is muscle-like, strong.
> The bones are wood within.
> The marrow is made resembling pith.[2]

Both these images of the human body establish a kinship between the self and the world of nature, establishing a world view that holds inherent respect for non-human realms of existence.

The *Atharva Veda*, the source of India's traditional medicine known as Ayurveda, includes passages in praise of the earth, asking for her beneficence and pledging protection in return. The text states "The earth is the mother, and I the son of the earth" (XII:12). The author attributes all wealth to the earth and appeals for her to be generous:

> The earth holds manifold treasures in secret places:
> wealth, jewels, and gold shall she give to me.
> She bestows wealth liberally; let that kindly
> goddess bestow wealth upon us! (XII:44).

Despite this yearning to benefit from her largesse, the author nonetheless harbors a desire not to hurt her, stating "What I dig out of thee, O earth, shall quickly grow again: may I not, O pure one, pierce thy vital spot, (and) not thy heart!" (XII:35). This plea indicates a sense of respect and care for the earth, expressing concern that the earth be made aware that the speaker will not hurt her. In yet another verse, the speaker states:

> Your snowy mountain heights, and your forests,
> O earth, shall be kind to us!
> The brown, the black, the red, the multi-colored,
> the firm earth that is protected by Indra,
> I have settled upon, not suppressed, not slain, not wounded (XII:11).

In recognition of mother earth's abundance, the *Atharva Veda* offers both praise of her power and assurances that she will not be harmed by human intervention.[3]

Throughout the Hindu religious tradition, rituals and ceremonies celebrate myriad manifestations of nature. Pilgrimages abound wherein pious folk trek to sacred places such as mountain tops and the confluence of rivers. Daily observances include the veneration of the five elements and the recitation of ancient hymns that extol their power. Families often do not partake of a meal until food has been shared with birds, who fly through the open windows to receive their offerings. Special trees are placed "under worship," such as the Bodhi Tree under which the Buddha achieved his enlightenment, and the Tulsi tree, a species beloved by and closely associated with the worship of Krishna. In these and countless other examples, a continuity is assumed between the human world and that of nature.

In this collective Hindu model, the human order is seen as an extension of and utterly reliant upon the natural order. As stated in the *Bhagavad Gītā*, the person of knowledge "sees no difference between a learned Brahmin, a cow, an elephant, a dog, or an outcaste."[4] According to the monistic Vedānta tradition, which will be discussed more fully in the next chapter, there is no fundamental difference between ourselves and others; both are undergirded by the common substrate known as Brahman. In the language of Vedānta, the Brahman is inseparable from its individual manifestations. To violate another creature is to violate Brahman itself. This ethos, signaling deep concern for harmony among life forms, has led to a minimal consumption of natural resources, particularly for members of religious orders.

A colleague once told me a story wherein a development worker was confronted with and confounded by nonviolence in the context of attitudes in India regarding the worth of animal life. It seems that several years ago, a major factor contributing to food shortages in India was the prevalence and voraciousness of the rodent population: a significant percentage of each year's grain crop was devoured by rats. An American was called in from a development agency to assess the situation. He immediately proposed poison. Shocked and affronted, his Indian co-workers asserted that such a solution simply would not be acceptable; to kill the rats would be in violation of *ahiṃsā*. After much discussion, a variety of alternatives were considered and one proved to be satisfactory for curtailing the rat population in the spirit of *ahiṃsā*. The grain storage facilities were placed on stilts, thus stymieing the vermin without directly injuring them.

In another demonstration of resourcefulness in using nonviolent techniques, a woman from India told me a story that occurred during her childhood in West Bengal. An important local temple had become overrun with ants. The offerings to the enshrined deity were being consumed, not by the god or the resident priests, but by swarms of industrious insects. To kill them was unthinkable, but their presence grew increasingly intolerable. Finally, one enterprising temple-goer proposed a solution that at first seemed preposterous but, due to lack of alternatives, was given a try. Next to the existing temple a new shrine was erected, to and for the ants. Rather than being composed of stone, this religious center was comprised solely of sugar cane, and included offerings of refined sugar. Soon, the human temple was free of pestilence and, judging by the numbers of devotees, the ant temple soon outstripped its human counterpart in popularity.

Aldo Leopold, in *A Sand County Almanac*, similarly tells of a noninjurious method of utilizing seemingly uninhabitable land. He draws a contrast between the American Southwest, where delicate grasslands have been ruined by overgrazing, and similar ecosystems in South Asia, noting that "in India, regions devoid of any sod-farming grass have been settled, apparently without wrecking the land, by the simple expedient of carrying the grass to the cow, rather than vice-versa."[5] Again, a very direct and simple method is used to preserve delicate interacting life forms.

Each of these anecdotes demonstrates common-sense methods of avoiding harm to living systems, whether they be insect, mammal, vegetation, or the earth itself.

Gandhi, Nonviolence, and Economic Environmentalism

A study of nonviolence in India would not be complete without reference to Mahatma Gandhi, who drew upon the existing tradition as learned primarily from Jainas (with input from Tolstoy and British vegetarians) to develop a campaign for national independence. It is not possible to fully explore here Gandhi's theories and applications of nonviolence, much of which pertain to political action. However, one phase of Gandhi's work does hold possible implications for a postmodern approach to the environment: his proposed revitalization of village economies, based on the principles of nonviolence (*ahiṃsā*) and nonpossession (*aparigraha*). The purpose of Gandhi's campaign was to make villages self-sufficient, able to cooperate through mutual trade without the importation of foreign produced goods. His means to achieve this was through spinning and weaving cloth and revitalizing other crafts within each village, requiring that schools include these skills as part of the curriculum. Although the aim of this program was to subvert the colonial economic dependence thrust upon India by the British, and despite the fact that Gandhi himself did not object to industrialization, the conservation of energy inherent in the system could be effectively used to counter some of the environment peril posed in the postmodern world.

Nonviolence, in the classical texts and traditions we have examined, is an ethical practice undertaken to lessen one's bondage and suffering; for the Jainas, it was considered to be the prime practice for expelling all karma and thereby achieving spiritual solitude (*kevala*). It necessitated an austere, simple lifestyle. For Mahatma Gandhi, steeped in the Indian climate of nonviolence and prompted into action by social oppression, nonviolence became a rallying point for a social movement. He observed that in order for nonviolence to be put into effect, it must not be limited to oneself. "To me virtue ceases to have any value if it is cloistered or possible only for individuals."[6] For Gandhi, the propriety of nonviolence has to be extended into the wider net of one's interrelationships:

> We have all along regarded the spinning wheel, village crafts, etc. as the pillars of ahiṃsā, and so indeed they are. They must stand. But we have not to go a step further. A votary of ahiṃsā will of course base upon nonviolence, if he has not already done so, all his relations with his partner, his children, his wife, servants, his dependents, etc. But the real test will come at the time of political or communal disturbances.... If I am a Hindu, I must fraternise with the Muslims and the rest. In my dealing with them I may not make any distinctions between co-religionists and those who might belong to a different faith.[7]

Gandhi did not separate the practice of nonviolence from economic realities. He wrote:

> I must confess that I do not draw a sharp or any distinction between economics and ethics. Economics that hurt the moral well-being of an individual or a nation are immoral and, therefore, sinful....True economics...stands for social justice, it promotes the good of all equally including the weakest, and is indispensable for decent life.[8]

For Gandhi, the most viable vehicle for equitable economics was the village, the millenia-old locus of India's intellectual as well as economic lifeblood:

> I believe that independent India can discharge her duty toward a groaning world only by adopting a simple but ennobled life by developing her thousands of cottages and living at peace with the world.[9]

He warned that the villages must be protected from the potential perils of mechanization, asserting that as the economic process becomes more complex, those at the lower end suffer:

> Industrialization on a mass scale will necessarily lead to passive or active exploitation of the villages as the problems of competition and marketing come in. Therefore, we have to concentrate on the village being self-contained.[10]

Gandhi envisioned a network of largely self-sufficient villages:

> My idea of village swaraj is that it is a complete republic, independent of its neighbors for its own vital wants, and yet inter-dependent for many others in which dependence is a necessity. Thus, every village's first concern will be to grow its own food crops and cotton for its clothes....My economic creed is a complete taboo in respect to all foreign commodities, whose importation is likely to prove harmful to our indigenous interests. This means that we may not in any circumstances import a commodity that can be adequately supplied from our country.[11]

Like the Jainas, Gandhi emphasized that livelihood must be undertaken with the least amount of violence possible:

> Strictly speaking, no activity and no industry is possible without a certain amount of violence, no matter how little. Even the very process of living is impossible without a certain amount of violence. What we have to do is to minimize it to the greatest extent possible. Indeed the very word non-violence, a negative word, means that it is an effort to abandon the violence that is inevitable in life. Therefore, whoever believes in *Ahiṃsā* will engage himself in occupations that involve the least possible violence.[12]

Again, the perceived means to accomplish this, according to Gandhi, was to be found at the village level.

> This land of ours was once, we are told, the abode of the Gods. It is not possible to conceive Gods inhabiting a land which is made hideous by the smoke and the din of mill chimneys and factories, and whose roadways are traversed by rushing engines, dragging numerous cars crowded with men who know not for the most part what they are after, who are often absent-minded and whose tempers do not improve by being uncomfortably packed like sardines in boxes and finding themselves in the midst of utter strangers who would oust them if they could and whom they would, in their turn, oust similarly. I refer to these things because they are held to be symbolic of material progress. But they add not an atom to our happiness.[13]

By minimizing one's needs and the means used to produce those needs, life, according to Gandhi, holds more potential for happiness.

These ideals are not found only in Gandhian analysis. E. F. Schumacher has also cited Buddhism as a tradition wherein the process of consumption is informed by higher values:

> While the materialist is mainly interested in goods, the Buddhist is mainly in liberation. But Buddhism is "The Middle Way" and therefore in no way antagonistic to physical well-being. It is not wealth that stands in the way of liberation but the attachment to wealth; not the enjoyment of pleasurable things but the craving for them. The keynote of Buddhist economics, therefore, is simplicity and non-violence. From an economist's point of view, the marvel of the Buddhist way of life is the utter rationality of its pattern—amazingly small means leading to extraordinarily satisfactory results.[14]

Schumacher has elaborated on this theme in *Small is Beautiful*, an eloquent plan for economic reorganization that drew significant attention during the 1970s. Although the present study does not allow for a full discussion of Schumacher's theories, a close parallel can be seen between his proposed paring-down of economic complexes and the traditional Indian virtues of nonviolence and minimalization of material possessions.[15] Schumacher makes a dramatic point that updates the traditional Indian concern for life in light of potential ecological disaster. To use up nonrenewable goods, a possibility inconceivable in classical India, is the ultimate form of violence, one that eventually diminishes both the number and varieties of life forms. Schumacher warns that caution must be exerted in the consumption process:

> Non-renewable goods must be used only if they are indispensable, and then only with the greatest care and the most meticulous concern for conservation. To use them heedlessly or extravagantly is an act of violence, and while complete non-violence may not be attainable on this earth, there is none the less an ineluctable duty on man to aim at the ideal of non-violence in all he does.[16]

As never before, humans now possess the ability to use, abuse, and ultimately destroy our own ecosystem.

Environmentalism in Contemporary India

We have explored a few aspects of India's long history of regard for human life, and we have seen examples of the great care which has been taken to preserve and protect life in its many forms. However, if we look at other aspects of Indian civilization, the converse is also true, particularly in regard to contemporary attitudes towards industrialization. During a trip to Kerala a few years ago I was stunned by the rampant pollution caused by the chemical manufacturers. We had spent a couple of hours traveling by bus to the birthplace of Śaṅkara when, all of a sudden, the lush, verdant landscape gave way to brown stubble and the sweet tropical air became foul with chemical stench, revealing the worst of what one encounters in New Jersey or Niagara Falls. We approached the plant—ironically a producer of fertilizer—and were "welcomed" by a dour crowd of employees, who seemed none-too-thrilled with their factory-dominated existence. As we pulled away from the plant, I commented to one of our hosts that the pollution seemed extreme. He blithely replied that fortunately no one lived nearby. However, as we rounded a bend, a construction project was underway, well within the umbrella of foul air: new housing for factory workers. As we left the general locale and returned to the world of rice paddies, rickshaws, and coconuts, I could not help but fear for the long-term effects of apparently unregulated industry. A couple of years later, sadly, my sense of foreboding was confirmed: the Union Carbide disaster in Bhopal took the lives of over 3800 persons in central India.

During this trip to India in 1981, I was struck with the violence to the environment incurred in India by its burgeoning industrialization. The level of awareness in this regard was close to nonexistent, much to my consternation and distress. However, since that time, a noticeable change has taken place: virtually every newspaper routinely includes a story of environmental interest nearly every day. One possible reason for the willingness of the Indian press to lend credibility to the environmental cause is that the head of the *Times of India*, the leading daily, Ashok Jain, is himself a member of the Jaina community.[17]

Since the Bhopal Union Carbide disaster, two major centers have been established to serve as clearinghouses for environmental issues. In New Delhi, the Centre for Science and Environment, in addition to other activities, provides a news service that supplies India's many newspapers with stories of environmental and ecological interest. In Ahmedabad, the Centre for Environment Education, located at the Nehru Foundation for Development, was established in 1984. It conducts an array of programs designed to enhance the general public's awareness of environmental issues. While in the city of Ahmedabad, home to many Jainas and the residence of Mahatma Gandhi for two decades, I visited with Meena Raghunathan, special programs officer of the Centre for Environment Education. It offers workshops and produces materials that reach over ten thousand teachers per year. It operates the "News and Features Service," similar to that of the Centre for Science and Environment. It has initiated a rural education program to help stem the destruction of India's remaining forests. It conducts various urban programs, including the promotion of the smokeless *chulha*, or woodburning stove, for cooking.[18] In 1986 it launched the Ganga Pollution Awareness Programme, which has been widely documented in the United States. In cooperation with the School of Forestry of the State University of New York, located in Syracuse, it produced a series of environmental films for children. It has developed interpretive materials for the National Zoological Park in Delhi and for Kanha National Park. Within the city of Ahmedabad, it has installed a permanent ecological exhibit at Gujerat University; maintains a bird sanctuary at Sundarvan, its fourteen-acre campus; and has developed exhibits for the Gandhi Ashram.[19]

Another institution that has long been attuned to environmental concerns is the Gandhi Peace Foundation in New Delhi. Gandhi's village-based economic model, which was discussed earlier, may be seen as an early paradigm for the bioregionalism that many eco-activists promote today. Gandhi also criticized industrial development in a style quite remininiscent of Thoreau at Walden Pond, as we have seen. Reflecting the influence of his Jaina neighbors and advisors, he proposed a solution to the twin problems of industrialization and alienation by advocating that every occupation work at the minimization of violence. In addition to promoting and restating the works of Gandhi, the Gandhi Peace Foundation has engaged in various projects to promote village-based economies. It has encouraged farmers to grow food for themselves in addition to cultivating the usual cash crop. In cooperation with the Centre for Rural Development and Appropriate Technology of the Indian Institute of Technology, it has promoted the implementation of organic farming according to the model of Masanobu Fukuoka, who advocates no tilling or weeding, and no use of synthetic fertilizers or herbicides.[20] Although still in its rudimentary phases, T. S. Ananthu, a research associate, has spoken of the foundation promoting this program elsewhere in India.

Several movements in India have taken direct action in an effort to bring attention to enviromental concerns. The Chipko movement in Uttar Pradesh involves local women saving trees by embracing them, staving off bulldozers.[21] In traditional Indian folk culture, the tree is sacred, and intimately tied to survival of the land and its people. Vandana Shiva, a defender and spokesperson for the Chipko movement, tells the following story in this regard:

> Chipko started in the Himalayas...the source of the Ganges River....The Ganges was a mother goddess, and here were prayers for her to be brought to earth....She couldn't just come because her power was so strong that if she landed on earth, she would just destroy. It's really symbolic of the way we get our monsoon rain. It comes so strong, so powerful, that if we don't have forest cover, we get landslides and floods. So, the god Shiva had to be requested to help in getting the Ganges down to earth. And Shiva laid out his hair, which was very matted, to break the force of the descent of the Ganga. Shiva's hair is basically seen by a lot of us in India as a metaphor for the vegetation and forests of the Himalayas.
>
> That's the sort of concept people in India have constantly. And so when they see forests cut, they see the god's tresses being violated. When they see the Ganges being dammed, they see their sacred river being violated. When Indian movements live for a long time, they are very heavily based on these sorts of concepts.[22]

The Chipko movement, whose name means "to embrace," traces its origins to 1913, when there was a major movement to protect forest lands. It became revitalized in 1977 with a group of women in the Himalayan region who tied sacred threads and formed chains around trees in order to prevent their harvest. Women who dwell in forested areas have for millenia lived in close relationship with trees; the forest provides fodder, fertilizer, food, water, and fuel. The cutting of forests for purposes of monoculture interrupts this ecological balance, and has caused great devastation in various parts of India. Although men are involved with Chipko, trees and their protection have long been identified with women in India. Vandana Shiva notes that in Hinduism

> All the nature deities are always female, by and large, because all of them are considered *prakṛti*, the female principle in Hindu cosmology. Also, all of them are nurturing mothers—the trees feed you, the streams feed you, the land feeds you, and everything that nurtures you is a mother.[23]

She tells the story of one woman who battled the development of a quarry, which was proposed at the expense of a vast expanse of forest. The contractor had hired two hundred men to harass the demonstrators, who refused to leave, despite being beaten and pelted with stones. When asked "What is it in you that gives you all this *shakti* (strength)?," the friend replied:

> "Can you see all this grass growing? We come to cut this grass and every year it grows back. And the power in that grass is the power in me. Do you see these trees growing? They are two hundred years old. Every year we lop these trees to feed our cattle and to keep our children alive, so that the children have milk, and still the trees keep growing and still keep nurturing us, and that shakti is in me. See this stream? Every year the rain comes, and it could just run off every year, but these trees stay alive long after the rain goes, and they keep feeding us. Clear sparkling water better than anything you get in the cities, and I call it living water. Your water you get in the cities is dead; it comes from a tap. This living water gives me life. And that's my shakti."[24]

This anecdote shows the simple beauty of a naturally ecological lifestyle, one that is assaulted by increasing urbanization and Western-style "development."

Vandana Shiva explicitly attacks the premises of third world development projects in her book, *Staying Alive*, an eloquent appeal to reverse the drive for world homogenization based on the Western model. In addition to a more standard feminist critique, she also develops a theory of nature rooted in *prakṛti* and *shakti*, thus utilizing conceptual resources indigenous to Indian tradition. She points out that development policies often entail a shift from holistic, ecologically sound subsistence farming largely conducted by women to cash-crop farming of one product, often enhanced by technology, that is dominated by men. She refers to this practice as "maldevelopment," stating that "it ruptures the co-operative unity of masculine and feminine, and places man, shorn of the feminine principle, above nature and women, and separated from both....Nature and women are turned into passive objects, to be used and exploited for the uncontrolled and uncontrollable desires of alienated man."[25] She contrasts the instantiated immediacy of *prakṛti*, in which all things are viewed as part of a living continuum, with the deadness of things other than human as perceived in the Cartesian-scientific-technological model, wherein they are regarded only for their potential to be transformed into consumable goods. She criticizes the manipulation of seed technology and the development of inorganic fertilizers as potentially harmful to India's ecosystem.

Baba Amṭe, winner of the 1990 Templeton Prize for Progress in Religion, has focused resistance to the Narmada River Valley dam project by conducting a vigil unto death in protest of the planned destruction by flooding of over 325,000 acres of forest and agricultural land in western India. The first Asian to win the United Nations Human Rights Award, Baba Amte is best known for his pioneering work on behalf of India's lepers. Following the Bhopal disaster of 1984 that claimed over 3800 lives, he began an environmental campaign, stating that "It is this invisible leoprosy of greed and ambition that is turning our world into a wasteland."[26] His work on behalf of environmental causes has taken him to villages directly affected by the Narmada River Valley and other super-dam projects, somewhat reminiscent of Gandhian grassroots movements.

Jaina Environmentalism

During a visit in 1989 to Jain Vishva Bharati in Ladnun, a small desert town in western Rajasthan, I met with Acharya Tulsi, who has served as the head of the Terāpanthi Śvetāmbara (Jaina) sect since 1936.[27] I inquired as to whether the Jaina religion is responding to the current ecological crisis. His response was very much in the style of traditional Indian pedagogy. He spoke not of political or legislative action (though I did ask him about such matters) but rather referred to his own lifestyle. He showed me what he owns: his white robes, his eating utensils, and his personal collection of books. The latter can only be read with a magnifying glass: copies of the primary Jaina *sūtras* and the original 250-year-old document establishing his order have been rendered in tiny print, so as to allow easy transport. The life of a Jaina monk or nun is a life of homelessness. While in Ladnun, Acharya Tulsi occupies the corner of a classroom at Jain Vishva Bharati; there is no place and very few things that he can call his own. In a very direct way, he was in fact showing me the most radical form of ecological lifestyle: no automobile, no house, few clothes. Nonpossession (*aparigraha*), one of the five requirements for Jaina living, eschews attachment to any thing.

The work of Acharya Tulsi, in many ways akin to Gandhianism but largely free from a political agenda, has had a long history in India. On March 1, 1949, he instituted the Anuvrat movement, a series of twelve vows that he urges persons to take, ranging from the vow of *ahiṃsā*—"I will not kill any innocent creature"—to the twelfth, which states "I will do my best to avoid contributing to pollution."[28] The premise of this program is that the transformation of society must begin with transformation of the individual. S. Gopalan states that Acharya Tulsi "emphasizes the fact that the ills of society automatically get cured by means of the process of self-purification and self-control."[29] Sarvepalli Radhakrishnan, the former philosopher-president of India, in support of the Anuvrat movement wrote

> There is a general feeling in the country that while we are attending to the material progress and doing substantial work in that direction, we are neglecting the human side of true progress. A civilized human being must be free from greed, vanity, passion, anger. Civilizations decline if there is a coarsening of moral fibre, if there is callousness of heart. Man is tending to become a robot, a mechanical instrument caring for nothing except his material welfare, incapable of exercising his intelligence and responsibility. He seems to prefer comfort to liberty....to remedy this growing indiscipline, lack of rectitude, egotism, the Anuvrat Movement was started on March 1, 1949. It requires strict adherence to the principles of good life.[30]

The goal of the Anuvrat movement, which is now over forty years in process, is to encourage persons to adapt their lifestyle to effect a more nonviolent world. Gandhi employed a similar technique in his Satyagraha campaigns. The current ecological drive towards bioregionalism, with its emphasis on local concerns, bears similarity to both Gandhi's and Acharya Tulsi's models.

This approach to environmental ethics teaches that environmental ravage arises due to over-consumption. By minimizing consumption, one minimizes harm to one's environment. However stark the life of Acharya Tulsi may be, Jainism does not mandate that all Jainas must follow the life of a monk. Jaina laypersons have long been challenged by the example of the monk to make their own lifestyles less violent, as indicated in the illustration of the pharmaceutical company's release of test animals back into the wild. The frugality of the Jainas also underscores a concern to minimize the diminishment of one's resources.

We have surveyed three Indian approaches aimed at correcting the current ecological assault: efforts at general education, as seen with the Centre for Science and Environment and the Centre for Environment Education; the direct action of the Chipko movement and Baba Amte; and changing one's own lifestyle, as advocated by the example of Acharya Tulsi. The Gandhi Peace

Foundation seemingly combines all three aspects. Each of these is rooted in a uniquely Indian orientation and each has demonstrated a degree of success, though perhaps not easily discernable by Euro-American standards. For each of these, unlike in the West, there is no need to "redo" traditional theology to make it ecological. The purest of models is perhaps the third, held forth by Jaina monastics, who own virtually nothing, who will not even as much as touch a leaf, who tend to stay in the desert so that natural life forms will not be disturbed. The first and second models, focusing on education and direct action, are perhaps more "Western" in approach, at least on the surface. One notable cultural difference, however, is that there seems to be less concern for legislative lobbying in India. When pressed on this issue, the standard response was that "In India, people do not pay attention to laws; the consciousness must be changed." This basic orientation has not strayed far from Gandhian and traditional religious models.

In many ways the current lifestyle of India contains elements that support an environmental perspective. Most persons live within a short scooter ride or walking distance of work. Foodstuffs consumed by Indians are comprised of grains purchased in bulk from the market and cooked with vegetables procured from traveling greengrocers who push their carts through virtually every neighborhood all day long. Waste is collected and used for fertilizer.

Yet all of this may soon change. In Delhi, I was served yogurt in a disposable plastic container. Private automobiles have begun to proliferate. The advent of a consumer economy seems to be eroding the possibility for an ecologically sound form of development. Although industrialization and technologicalization of the subcontinent are modest by American standards, the sheer numbers of people entering into the middle class make it difficult for the same mistakes of Western development to be avoided. One small example is the automobile: India now produces its own small cars, and increasingly they are owned by individuals. By some accounts (and by personal experience) the Delhi area has perhaps the most polluted air in the world. Yet these newly produced vehicles have no emissions controls, nor does there seem to be an interest in lobbying for them.

And yet as the general awareness of environmental ravage increases, even here in the United States, the best and most cutting-edge solutions seem to follow the model proposed by Acharya Tulsi in India. It is only when each individual makes a change in his or her lifestyle that a societal leap forward can occur. In America, the seeds of this transformation have been sown; over 80 percent of the populace define themselves as "environmentalists," indicating that concern for ecological harmony has been widely accepted. Americans now are educating themselves on how not to use the fabulous technology available to them, from household chemicals to nuclear weapons.

In India, people traditionally have not been divorced from the earth: to think of themselves as separate from the ongoing and all-pervasive cycle of life and death would be inconceivable. And yet now India and its religious traditions face the challenges of modernity, technology, consumerism, and technological ravage; in short, buying into the American dream where the world and one's relationship to it become estranged and objectified. Part of the solution to ecological ravage requires the hard work of scientists, technocrats, and educators, those responsible for inventing and inculcating the values of consumer society. However, we need also to look off the wheel, so to speak; we need to get out of the car to fix it. For this, the example set by the renouncers of India who advocate minimal consumption continues to offer a solution for myriad problems. By attacking the source of human misery through uprooting attachment itself, a true type of peace that automatically extends to others can be fostered.

Environmental Concern in Buddhist Tradition

In our earlier discussion regarding the life of animals, it was established that according to the Jaina and Buddhist world views, life forms are interchangeable. Each person has been reborn so many myriad times that each being has at one time or another been a blood relation. Within the Jaina tradition, as noted in the first chapter, these life forces or *jīva* that eventually may assume human form, are found in the earth and other elements, in microoganisms, and in plants as well as in animals and humans, leading some early scholars to characterize the Jaina tradition as "animism." Due to this biocosmology, Jainism developed the assiduous practices of nonviolence mentioned earlier and advocated somewhat successfully that these practices be adopted by others. Hence, although Hinduism did not abandon its commitment to Vedāntic monism or the twenty-five-fold Sāṃkhyan analysis, and while Buddhism did not abandon its commitment to no-self, suffering, and impermanence, both traditions came to cherish the practice of nonviolence, which became the primary ethical precept common to all three traditions. Despite differing fundamental world views, orthopraxy established common ground. And, in an interesting and indirect fashion, the piece of Jaina cosmology that declares plants sacred and forbids its monks and nuns from touching them lest they be harmed, reemerges in China and Japan with the proclamation that the plant world has Buddha-nature.

Chi-tsang (549–623 C.E.) wrote in the *Ta-ch'eng-hsüan-lun* that "in theory plants and trees, since they are essentially like sentient beings, can achieve Buddhahood."[31] Although this idea was certainly not accepted by all Chinese

Buddhist thinkers and was also criticized by the twelfth-century Japanese monk Shoshin,[32] it became a key theme in Noh drama of the Muromachi period, wherein "the medieval Japanese audience saw the spirits of bizarre and exotic plants like the moonflower or banana plant ecstatically dancing out the joy of their liberation."[33] Whereas the Jainas would require that the tree be reborn and eventually incarnated as a human person before *kevala* could be achieved, in East Asian tradition, the plant or tree itself is said to enter *nirvāṇa.* It might be argued that in a state of enlightenment one would see plants and trees as not different from oneself and hence also enlightened. In either case, the insight is uniquely ecological: plants and trees, it would seem, are to be valued as intrinsically worthy of veneration and protection.

In the *Yü-Li* ("Precious Records") of the Sung dynasty, cited earlier as an example of the Chinese adherence to the Buddhist doctrine of noninjury to animal life, several instances are given wherein to treat the environment poorly is regarded as being as serious an offense as the mistreatment of animals. In one instance, a wealthy man sets a mountainside on fire in order to eliminate its many tigers and other animals. But then his own son sets his father's house on fire, proclaiming "I am the son of a serpent whom you killed with myriads of other creatures when you fired the mountain side."[34] This story links the animal realm with the larger natural order.

Destructive technology used to enhance food production is also criticized:

> There was a very large fish-pond to the north of Lo Shin, and once a year the natives sacrificed to the god of the pool. Some person taught the fishermen to poison the water in the stream above and they would be able to catch ten times the quantity of fish. The method was adopted with success. One day about noon a terrible storm arose and it thundered, and all the huts of the fishermen were burnt. This put a fear upon the people.[35]

In this interesting tale, nature herself punishes those who abuse her. In another story, a lad died shortly after having defiled well water with manure.[36] Although more anecdotal than systematic, these tales nonetheless testify to a concern for maintaining the natural order, pointing out dire consequences for those who abuse either earth or water.

Modern American Buddhists have linked Buddhism's principles of interpenetration with the ecological view that all life forms are interconnected. Joan Halifax writes:

> In contemporary Buddhism, the term *Sangha* refers to the community that practices the way together. I have often asked myself,

> Where is the boundary of this community? From the perspective of some tribal peoples, Sangha does not stop at the threshold of our species and next of kin. Community for many native peoples is regarded as including other species, plant and animal, as well as environmental features and unseen ancestors and spirits. Community is lived and experienced as a whole system of interrelated types and species. Most importantly, this community is alive, all of it.[37]

The Buddhist notion of the nonsubstantiality of an independent self or essense is seen as key to the adoption of a truly ecological perspective, as noted by Padmasiri de Silva:

> The day to day maintenance of our life support system is dependent on the functional interactions of countless interdependent biotic and physiochemical factors. Since the inherent value of life is a core value in Buddhist ethical codes, the notion of reciprocity and interdependence fits in with the Buddhist notion of a causal system. A living entity cannot isolate itself from this causal nexus, and has no essence of its own. Reciprocity also conveys the idea of mutual obligation between nature and humanity, and between people.[38]

Buddhism when regarded in this light is seen as actively involved with and interested in so-called worldly matters, in contrast to its rather unfortunate characterization as "world-denying or even world-loathing."[39]

German Buddhologist Lambert Schmithausen has argued that the protection accorded to animals indicates that wider networks of life systems should also be protected. He states that

> In the morality of renouncers and ascetics, abstention from killing animals (and even plants) was firmly rooted as the heritage of an earlier cultural stratum—a stratum in which killing animals (and even plants, earth and water) was, in a sense at least, as serious as killing people (not of course of one's own ethnic group), because animals, too, were believed to take, if possible, revenge on the killer in the yonder world (or to be avenged by their kin here itself). The very idea of animals taking revenge...would seem to indicate a kind of social relationship with them. In the case of a renouncer and ascetic living in the wilderness (*araṇya*) one may even say that it is primarily the wild animals (and plants) that constitute his society, so to speak....From this point of view it

> seems that also in the first Precept, and hence also for a Buddhist lay person, society is not to be taken in the narrow sense of human society, but in a broader sense of a community comprising all living or sentient beings, including, at any rate, the animals....Later texts occasionally express, in the context of motivating universal compassion and benevolence, the idea that all sentient beings are to be regarded as the self, or as equal to oneself, and try to establish a metaphysical basis for this either in the doctrine of the nonexistence of a self (i. e. a substantial Ego) or in the presence of a common "self" or true essence of all sentient beings.[40]

Schmithausen, having acknowledged that the first Precept (*pāṇātipātā paṭivirato hoti*) does not allow killing, and assenting to the later interpretations that extend the prohibition to protect the lives of plants, struggles to reconcile the difficulty of its observance with contemporary life. He writes:

> Probably, the most honest way is to accept the uncomfortable truth that one's own survival is possible only at other living beings' expense, but to try one's best to reduce the damage to a minimum. Perhaps, to live as a vegetarian (whenever possible). But what is, to my mind, much more important is to oppose and boycott, especially as consumers, all forms of cruelty to animals and destruction or deterioration of ecosystems. E.g., not to buy meat or eggs if the animals have been reared under unnatural or even cruel conditions. Not to buy fish if the fishing is done in an unnecessarily cruel or in an insane, immoderate way, depleting the oceans, as e.g. driftnet fishing does....Not to buy wasteful products....Not to spoil the beauty of nature by carelessly dropping rubbish. To use polluting engines like cars...as rarely as possible and rather take the train...or the bicycle. To join or support organizations protecting nature.[41]

Schmithausen's remarks have been met with controversy in Japan, where Buddhologist N. Hakamaya disagrees with Schmithausen's assessment, claiming that "Buddhism does not accept but negates nature,"[42] and warns against animistic interpretations of the tradition.

In Thailand, Theravada Buddhist monks are taking direct action in order to stave off the clear cutting of forests through a highly unusual but effective means: they are ordaining trees, transforming them into Buddhist monks like themselves, thus detering loggers from chopping them down. One such monk, Phra Prachak, attributes his environmental commitment to the intimacy with the forest that he developed during his wanderings, noting that "I learned what this body is, that it is part of the forest."[43] Also within Thailand, Chatsumarn Kabilsingh has developed a Buddhist environmental school curriculum with support from the World Wildlife Fund.[44]

Jaina Cosmology and Gaia Theory

This brings us to an interesting methodological question. Is it appropriate or useful to employ an ethical principle that arises from a specialized religious community of renouncers to address modern issues that arise from a radically different world view? We have seen that Jaina principles would strongly support an ecological ethic. However, to what extent would the Jaina perspective be useful for application to a problem that stems from an utterly foreign, scientific and technological world view?

If one is unwilling to question the presuppositions that have led to ecological demise, then the concepts underlying the theory and practice of *ahiṃsā* would be useless, and it would be meaningless to follow Jaina prohibitions against harming life forms. However, the environmental movement does in fact critique the premise that the earth was created for humans to exploit, as noted in the ground-breaking article by Lynn White.[45] The world view that created disturbances to the ecosystem has been called into question. Furthermore, proponents of the Gaia theory claim that the earth itself lives and breathes, rejecting the notion that the earth as we know it consists primarily of inert matter.

The Gaia theory is one of two new Western models proposed in response to this questioning of both the philosophical and the scientific presuppositions that allowed humankind to exploit nature mercilessly for its own purposes. Both this scientific model and the other, a theological model, can be readily adapted to support an ecological orthopraxy akin to that practiced by Jainas. The scientific model was first suggested under the title "biogeochemistry" by Vladimir I. Vernadsky, and later developed by James E. Lovelock, who dubbed it the Gaia theory, and Lynn Margulis, who is conducting research to help prove the hypothesis. The Gaia theory, as we will see, claims that many of the objects that in prior times were considered inanimate are in fact the by-products of biological processes. The theological model is known as panentheism, which literally means "everything in God." The term was first used by K. F. C. Krause in the nineteenth centurty, and has recently been reintroduced by process theologians. It emphasizes the presence of deity within each of its manifestations. Panentheism suggests that the world is a dynamic expression of God's creation, a "self-conscious Life within whom the unfoldings of the universe occur," and that human beings need to respect and protect the earth accordingly.[46] Although each of these differs significantly from Jainism, both give credence to the general Jaina claim that life extends beyond the obvious domains of plants and animals, and that steps need to be taken to assure that life systems are not unduly harmed.

Due to its similarities with the Jaina theory of life, we will briefly survey the history of the Gaia hypothesis and discuss its possible ethical implications in light of Jaina ethics. Vernadsky (1863–1945) is considered the father of a discipline known as biogeochemistry,[47] the predecessor of the Gaia hypothesis. Biogeochemistry posits a link between the formation of the earth and the processes of life. James Lovelock first formulated his version of the Gaia theory when NASA asked him in the 1960s to establish criteria by which life could be detected on other planets. He discovered that the atmosphere of earth differs radically from that of other planets in our solar system, and suggested that the best way to determine if life exists elsewhere in the universe is to determine the specific chemical composition of distant atmospheres. He then began to question what makes our atmosphere so different, and came to the conclusion that life itself produced our unusual array of gases. Specifically, millions of years ago, bacteria on earth ate and digested rocks. In the process, they removed carbon dioxide from the atmosphere, thereby producing new forms of limestone and releasing nitrogen and oxygen into the atmosphere. Without the presence of bacteria, none of the world as we know it could exist today.

Lovelock emphasizes that the many geological formations and in fact the air itself are not dead matter but part of the dynamic processes of a living system:

> Somehow both geologists and biologists have failed to note that their separate researches have clearly demonstrated that the world is massively affected by the presence of life. The air we breathe, the oceans and the rocks are all either direct products of living organisms [think of the chalk cliffs of Dover, just one gigantic pile of shells] or else they have been greatly modified by their presence, and this even includes the igneous rocks coming from volcanos. Indeed organisms are not just adapting to a dead world determined by physics and chemistry textbooks alone, they live with a world that is the breath and the bones and the blood of their ancestors and they themselves are now sustaining.[48]

He regards our planetary system to be like a living system. Each piece performs a particular function that allows other parts to flourish. One system's garbage provides food for another.[49]

In considering Gaia theory, certain similarities arise with the Jaina system. First, both see all life as interconnected. No single form of life can be considered without acknowledgment of an infinite web of life forms. The air we breathe, to which we owe our life, consists of gases that were produced by other life forms. Both systems emphasize recognition of interdependence. The Gaia hypothesis posits a relationship between the earth's atmosphere and the rocks that formed as the bacteria did their work. In turn, plants, animals, and humans need the atmosphere and each other to survive. Life forms cannot exist in isolation. The Jainas posit that the *jīvas,* or life forces, pervade the earth and its atmosphere. They undergo an unending process of transmutation, with the decay of one form giving birth to a new one.

Neither the Gaia hypothesis nor Jainism is apocalyptic. Jainism does not speak of the end of the world, only a rearrangement of its pieces and possible liberation for its most elevated monastic members. Proponents of the Gaia theory dismiss the notion that life on our planet will be obliterated by human interference. Rather, they claim that it might be severely mutated, but that some species, especially cockroaches and bacteria, will survive even the most horrid of environmental debacles.[50] Consequently, proponents of Gaia theory explicitly criticize as excessively anthropocentric the Teilhardian notion that humans are the pinnacle of the creation process, marching onward toward a final beatific state.[51] Lynn Margulis warns that if we do not take full responsibility for the production of all sorts of human wastes (including the chemicals that currently endanger the ozone layer) and if we do not curb our reproductive rate, the survival of human life as we know it is imperiled.

Both Gaia thought and Jainism raise issues of an ethical nature. Jainas, as we have seen, have developed nonviolent lifestyles stemming from their deep regard for all living beings and elements. By comparison, the ethics implied by Gaia is unformed, though an ethic that mandates reducing harm to the environment seems inescapable, as suggested by Margulis. Human beings share a development of conscience and a consciousness enriched by subtle emotions and deep memories; presumably these two qualities distinguish humans from the millions of other species that have taken birth on earth. According to Jaina philosophy, human persons can dissipate themselves in search of sensual gratification, but they can also reverse these tendencies, gain mastery over past karma, and actively pursue a life of nonviolence. In the process, they become nonspeciesistic and minimally intrusive on the environment.

The environmentalist lifestyle, advocated and practiced by many proponents of Gaia theory, is in many ways similar to the Jaina emphasis on recognizing the wider effects of one's activities. Both ancient Jainism and modern Gaia theory can be harnessed to support a contemporary environmentalist lifestyle. Individuals must account for the miles they drive and the garbage they consume in such a way that they are conscious of the extent and repercussions of their consumption of natural resources. Just as Jainas developed their sequence of five vows to prevent and reduce the destruction of living forms, so also vows not to pollute by minimizing purchases and recycling materials serve as approximate equivalents to Jaina monasticism.

Select vows of Jainism, interpreted with a bit of imagination, can easily be put to the service of ecologically sound living. The first vow, *ahiṃsā*, requires respect for and protection of all life forms, stemming from the premise that even a blade of grass is not different from oneself in its essential vitality. Advocates of vegetarianism claim that abstention from eating meat not only spares the lives of animals, but also helps contribute to a healthy ecosystem.[52] The third vow, not stealing, means that one abstains from taking what does not belong to oneself. This can be particularly instructive for peoples of the "developed world" who continue to consume the majority of the world's resources, spewing forth pollution as a primary byproduct. The fourth vow, that of nonpossession, is tacitly environmental, as demonstrated by Acharya Tulsi. The less one owns, the less harm has been committed to one's ecosphere. On a practical level, the fifth vow, sexual restraint, can be seen as one way to hold down population growth. Psychologically, it can be used as an exercise in post-patriarchal interpersonal relations, in which regarding other bodies as potential objects for sexual gratification or the seeing of others as manipulable is transformed into seeing other people and other people's bodies as not different from oneself.

These examples suggest a few ways in which the ancient Asian nonviolent ethic can be reinterpreted in light of the contemporary environmental crisis. However, in order for people to be sufficiently motivated to change their lifestyles, they would have to respond to the environment in such a way that they would regard it as a living, breathing system, the balance of which is essential to their own health and well being. In short, they would have to respond to the Gaia concept, panentheism, or some reasonable equivalent with the same psychic responsiveness that has characterized the success of traditional mythological and symbolic systems. A new form of environmental orthopraxy, not unlike the Jewish system of Kosher food, is needed, wherein some goods are avoided or recycled. Some examples were cited above by Schmithausen. Such actions can be seen as rituals that integrate a person into a wider ecosystem.

Thomas Berry has noted that much of the erosion of the earth's ecosystem is due to increasingly industrialized technology and expansion of transportation networks. Both of these take natural resources, convert them into "consumables," transport them across continents, and quickly process them into garbage.[53] Although the problem of environmental decay was not articulated during the time of Gandhi, the solutions that he proposed to counter the ills of colonialism can also be put into effect to redress this new and ultimately equally deleterious situation. The observance of nonviolence, coupled with a commitment to minimize consumption of natural resources, can contribute to restoring and maintaining an ecological balance.

Part II

The Nonviolent Self

Chapter 4

Otherness and Nonviolence in the Mahābhārata

We have now examined several aspects of *ahiṃsā* practice: its possible origins, its articulation in Jainism and Buddhism, and some possible applications to the modern issues of animal rights and environmentalism. Although we have touched briefly upon its appearance in Hindu tradition, we have not extensively discussed its usage beyond its mention in the Vedas, the Upaniṣads, and the *Yoga Sūtra.* In this chapter we will focus on one particular chapter from the *Mahābhārata* that provides a concise philosophical definition of *ahiṃsā* from a Hindu perspective. We have earlier referred to Vedāntic monism, the notion that all things share a fundamental sameness when viewed from the perspective of wisdom. In this chapter we will explore this concept as seen through the prism of *ahiṃsā*, applied to the story of the *Mahābhārata.*

The *Mahābhārata* story is reportedly told by a great seer (*ṛṣi*) named Kṛṣṇa Dvaipayana (not to be confused with Śrī Krishna), most commonly known as Vyāsa, to whom the four Vedas and all the Purāṇas are also attributed. The *Mahābhārata* is a story of staggering proportions, recounting the birth and death of a family and a people that is symbolic of the birth and death that touches all humankind. By looking at this story of the descendants of Vyāsa, one glimpses the totality of life: joy and tragedy, love and deceit, peace and war are all portrayed. A verse in the *Mahābhārata* says of itself: "Everything in the *Mahābhārata* is elsewhere. What is not there is nowhere."[1]

Each of the major characters of the epic stems from or in some way becomes related to Vyāsa, the teller of the epic. It is from Vyasa's seed that the story grows. The familial interconnectedness of these characters serves not only to underscore the drama and tragedy of the events with Oedipal grandeur, but also reveals an underlying tenet of the Indian world view: that we are all interconnected beings and need to more fully recognize and embody this fact. Theologically, this perspective can be traced to Upaniṣadic monism, the notion that there is a all-pervading higher reality out of which we are born and to which we will ultimately return. The unfolding of the epic in many ways mirrors the Hindu account of cosmic creation as articulated in the *Ṛg Veda* (10:129), the *Śatapatha Brāhmaṇa* (VI: 2. 2. 27), the *Bṛhadāraṇyaka Upaniṣad* (I:4), the *Chāndogya Upaniṣad* (3. 19, 6:2, etc.) as well as other texts. It tells how all things emerge from an indiscriminate chaos, the *asat*. From this chaos first arises the one. Through desire, this one first breaks in two and then multiplies, generating multifarious worlds. This process, the mode of *pravṛtti*, continues and then goes into the reverse: bit by bit the created world disintegrates. All particularities are lost and the world again returns to the *asat* (*pralaya* or *nivṛtti*), waiting perhaps to re-emerge.

In the life of an individual, the creation process takes place as one steps from the single state into marriage and responsibility, through the accomplishment of wealth (*artha*), pleasure (*kāma*), and righteousness (*dharma*) during the first two stages of life. The cycle is completed as one is weaned from the world one has issued forth, leaving it to one's children. One then returns to the forest (*vānaprastha*), to solitude and renunciation (*sannyāsa*), in anticipation of the final stage, the reabsorption into the *nirguṇa* realm. In the epic tale, Vyāsa is called forth to father two sons (plus a third, whose role is less central). These two multiply into 105, and further multiplication takes place. But then, tragically and unavoidably, as Krishna warns in the *Bhagavad Gītā*, all are destroyed, all enter into the final state of *pralaya*.

In a sense, this process is the cornerstone of all great epic texts: in tracing the birth, maturation, decline, and demise of a character or characters, a message is communicated that speaks to the condition of all beings. The epic medium, in its vast scope, gives one pause to consider more than the obvious. In reflecting on the struggles and joys and disappointments of the offspring of Vyāsa (who are both his literary and biological progeny) we are catching a glimpse of the cosmic flow of life which marks us all as humans. Yudhiṣṭhira, when asked by his father Dharma at the poisonous lake, "What is the greatest marvel?," replied that "each day, death strikes and we live as though we were immortal. That is what is the greatest marvel."[2]

During the story, the substance of Vyāsa divides into two opposing camps, the sons of Pāṇḍu and the sons of Dhṛtarāṣṭra; at this point, conflict and its seemingly impossible resolution become the constant theme in the

Mahābhārata. The two sets of cousins are locked in a struggle for sovereignty and wealth, due primarily to the weakness of greed. Duryodhana, head of the sons of Dhṛtarāṣṭra, wants what his cousins the Pāṇdavas have and entices one of them (Yudhiṣṭhira) to gamble it all away. Later Yudhiṣṭhira reveals to Draupadī, the wife of the five Pāṇdava brothers, that he succumbed to the challenge in hopes of winning the entire kingdom. The warring camps are of the same flesh and blood, having been reared as one family by the Grandsire Bhīṣma. To one another they are both self and other. At root, this is a story about self-identity and relationship with other. In the intertwined web of the Vyāsa lineage, each of the selves is also other; each of the others is also part of oneself. In the dharmic Pāṇḍavas there is much *adharma*—the battle is won only by treachery—and in the adharmic sons of Dhṛtarāṣṭra there is virtue; particularly in the tenacity exhibited by Duryodhana and his brother Dusśāsana. The apparently opposite is in fact seen to be the same; both originate from the same hidden yet omnipotent source.

The biological link of the primary characters is made amply clear. Even the truly other, the Rakṣāsas, the demons of the epic, become biologically linked through Hidimbi's seduction of Bhīma, one of the Pāṇḍavas, and the subsequent birth of Ghatotkatcha. Wherever they travel, the Pāṇḍavas find or make relations, in both the social and biological senses of the word. Krishna is linked to Arjuna through the marriage of Krishna's sister to Arjuna and the birth of the beloved Abhimanyu, whose son, rescued in utero by Krishna, ensures the continuity of life. In all major aspects of the story, the planting of seed ties peoples together.

Just as dualities of race are eliminated by marriage, another duality disintegrates in the collapse of the otherness of the sexes at critical junctures in the narrative. The rejected bride Amba becomes the warrior Śikhaṇḍin. Arjuna becomes a female impersonator. In contrast to the dependent role of Hindu women emphasized in later texts, Kuntī, Gāndhārī, and Draupadī emerge through their suffering and endurance in many ways stronger and wiser than the men upon whom they rely. Kuntī calls forth the gods to serve her when her husband is unable, and then shares her secret with her sister wife Madrī. Gāndhārī's renunciation of her eyesight shows amazing resolve and austerity (*tapas*). Draupadī plumbs the depths of Krishna's seeming duplicity when she declares "Sometimes the only way to protect dharma is to forget it. Ask Krishna. He knows."[3] Women exhibit great wisdom and power in this story.

The otherness of Karṇa, the secret son produced by an early union between Kuntī and the sun god, addresses universal issues of nature versus nurture: the special paradox he presents is of particularly tragic impact. The identity of Karṇa is unclear at first to all: he knows not who he is and thus knows not to whom he is other. His self is apparently defined by those who raised him, the "lowly" driver and his wife. Nonetheless, his royal, solar origins shine through; perhaps he is immediately recognized by Kuntī. But it is Duryodhana who embraces him, who establishes the nurturing relationship by offering acceptance and power to him. And it is to Duryodhana that Karṇa remains faithful, even after his bio/theological parentage and claim to the throne is revealed. The oldest of the sons of Kuntī, the hidden sixth brother, rejects his birthright and possible kingship out of loyalty to the one who offered welcome, while at the same time pledging to kill only one of Kunti's sons. His earthly life is split, he never becomes fully self nor fully other until the final moment.

The play of the *Mahābhārata*—and I use play in both senses of the word—begins in unity, with the single seed of Vyāsa. It splinters into dozens of pieces, the offspring of Pāṇḍu and Dhṛtarāṣṭra. The peaceful, solitary substance of the bearded ascetic is dissipated into the world of action and yet the origin, Vyāsa himself, like a Sāṃkhyika witness (*puruṣa*), stands outside, gazing over the entire affair with detachment and dispassion, isolated from the world of action and yet observing and recounting it. Each piece of himself is defined by both membership in one group and by otherness from the other. Ultimately the estrangement becomes fatally real, only then to be erased upon the final destruction of all members and the appearance of the final illusion. Much like the modern biological image of the dividing cell, the solitude of Vyāsa breaks into the realm of manifestation (*vyakta*), then through decrepitude and war is cast back into nothingness (*pralaya, avyakta*). One seed only remains: the son of Abhimanyu, Parikṣit, rejuvenated by Krishna to continue the story of humankind. Otherness and strife, so rampant in the text, stand in stark relief to the background origins of peace and pacification. Yet the two exist in reciprocity; they define one another. Without the tragedy of the battle, without the greed and treachery, deceit and disappointment, the story would be incomplete.

The illusion of otherness captivates the minds of Duryodhana and Yudhiṣṭhira and occasions the violence of the *Mahābhārata*. At first it is sublimated in the form of the dice game and then it is postponed through the thirteen years of exile. But finally the peace is shattered and, for one third of the epic, war consumes all. In reading the *Bhagavad Gītā*, which provides most people with their first introduction to the *Mahābhārata*, one could easily assume that the basic premise of Krishna's teaching glorifies war. Many a reader has winced when Krishna urges Arjuna to take up arms and Arjuna finally resolves to do so. A larger reading gives an utterly different picture: the war on Kurukṣetra becomes a holocaust wherein the winners find no enjoyment in their spoils and in fact are ultimately punished, at least temporarily, for their imprudent activities in war. Furthermore, the gruesomely graphic detail of battle presented in the narrative has the impact not of an advertisement to join the armed forces, but rather of an anti-war film that exhausts, repels, and instructs its viewers regarding the horrors of war. One yearns for resolution to this seemingly endless conflict, hopes that this might be a war to end all wars, a hope that ultimately is not found in the realm of winners and losers but in the realm that transcends both winning and losing, the dissolution of the veil of otherness and alienation. This place beyond both, revealed in the final scene, is a realm of pacification, where self and other become one, where the blind see, and all illusions are removed. It is to the other place, the place of pacification, peace, and nonviolence, to which our attention now turns.

The practice of nonviolence (*ahiṃsā*), as we have seen, is the basic requirement for religious life in Hinduism, Jainism, and Buddhism. It is called the greatest of dharmas. On his bed of arrows, the wise grand-uncle Bhīṣma offers instruction to Yudhiṣṭhira regarding this and other matters in chapter 114 of the Book of Teachings (*Anuśāsana Parvan*), the thirteenth book of the epic. The text of this brief chapter follows, which explains this practice in terms of both the physical abstention from committing harm and the perspective of seeing all things as one's self:

1. Yudhiṣṭhira said:
Nonviolence, Vedic dharma, meditation, control of the senses,
austerity, or service to the guru—
which of these is best for a person?

2. Bṛhaspati said: All these in all ways
are distinct doors of dharma. Listen indeed,
O Chief of the Bhāratas, as the six are praised.

3. Listen! I will speak of the unsurpassed,
the most excellent thing for a human:
the refuge of nonviolence,
the dharma which truly causes a man to succeed.

4. That person attains success
who has always reflected
on the three faults amongst all beings
and has controlled lust and anger.

5. The one who, desiring the pleasure of the self,
abstains from killing helpless animals with a stick,
would attain happiness.

6. That person who indeed sees beings as like his own self,
who has cast aside the stick

and whose anger is conquered,
prospers happily in the life to come.

7. Even the gods are bewildered at the path
of the one who seeks the abode of no abode,
who sees all beings
with the being of oneself as that of all beings.

8. From not holding to the other
as opposite from oneself
there is the essence of dharma;
the other proceeds (as other) due to desire.

9. In rejecting and giving, in pleasure and pain,
in the pleasant and the unpleasant,
the person who sees all things as the self goes to *samādhi.*

10. When the other strides among the others,
then the other strides in the other.
Let them imitate this indeed in the world of living beings;
by this skill, all dharma is taught.[4]

In this discourse, several interesting statements are made regarding the process of surrendering commitment to one's self-position in such a way that the other is not seen as different from oneself. This surrender of possessiveness is referred to as "the abode of no abode," a place where nothing is held as one's own, yet everything becomes one's own: "the being of oneself is seen as that of all beings. " The otherness of things, and the otherness of other beings dissolves, resulting in a state of *samādhi*, described in *Yoga Sūtra* I.41 as "like a clear jewel, with unity among grasper, grasping, and grasped. " With this jewel-like consciousness, wherever one goes, there the self is seen. Whomever one sees, there the self is seen. In such consciousness, violence becomes improbable. Who would want to do violence to oneself? "When the other strides among the others, then the other strides in the other" (XIII:114:10). In this usage of the word other (*para*) it clearly becomes interchangeable with the term itself; it also can mean highest self.

The *Mahābhārata* presents otherness with unparalleled drama. These words of nonviolence resonate in a battlefield littered with the stinking bodies of those who saw other as other, not self as other or other as self. Though literally of the same substance, the Pāṇḍava clan decimated the sons of Dhṛtarāṣṭra. The oneness of Vyāsa had become mired in otherness and hence self-destructed, leaving behind only one baby to continue. Multiplicity is eliminated not through a wisdom gained by understanding and knowledge, but by enduring the ravages of life and war and death. The battle that obliterates and liberates all is a battle of pain and sorrow.

Krishna in the *Mahābhārata* might be seen as little more than a warlord who desires the dissolution of the world for some mysterious, inarticulated reason discovered only in the final scene. On the one hand, this seems to be true: Krishna sees the battle as inevitable. In fact, it does serve to purify the world. However, the great leaders of both sides dread the coming of the war and the anguish it will bring. The images conjured in anticipation sicken everyone. Arjuna's hesitation and despondence in the first chapter of the *Bhagavad Gītā* is perhaps the most famous example. Duryodhana, for years, suffers nightmares over the coming war. Karṇa laments its inevitability, as indicated in Carrière's dramatic adaptation:

> Flesh and blood rain from the sky.
> Bodiless voices cry in the night.
> Horses weep. One-eyed, one-legged
> monstrosities hop across the land.
> Birds perch on flags with fire in their beaks
> crying "Ripe! It's ripe!"
> A cow gives birth to an ass,
> a woman to a jackal.
> Newborn babies dance.
> Sons learn to be men between their mothers' thighs.
> Statues write with their weapons.
> Torches no longer give light.
> Cripples laugh. The different races merge.
> Vultures come to prayer.
> The setting sun is surrounded by disfigured corpses.[5]

Likewise, Yudhiṣṭhira is reluctant, though it was his greed for the entire kingdom that precipitated the disastrous dice game. This error led to his chastisement by Draupadī, which prompted his resolve to wage war. But throughout he bemoans the tragedy of it all, expressing even during the forest exile that one person's victory is another's defeat. When his father Dharma, having taken his brothers' lives at the mysterious poison lake, asks Yudhiṣṭhira for an example of defeat, Yudhiṣṭhira replies, "Victory." And again when Dharma asks, "What is your opposite?," Yudhiṣṭhira answers "Myself."[6] Yet despite his insight and despite the hesitation of the other warriors, the war is played out to its gruesome conclusion. Players and audience alike are dragged along.

The origins of the *Mahābhārata* war, like the origins of creation, are found in desire. Duryodhana and Yudhiṣṭhira desire what the other has, without seeing the other as self. This bifurcation of consciousness, dramatically played out to its ignominious conclusion, ultimately collapses with the death of the characters: the sons of Dhṛtarāṣṭra, then the sons of the Pāṇḍavas, and finally the five Pāṇḍavas themselves. When first acquainted with this tale many years ago, it annoyed me that it did not end with Yudhiṣṭhira and his brothers living happily ever after. It further shocked and puzzled me that the Pāṇḍavas landed in hell. These misgivings were indeed shared by a troop of European scholars, including Oldenberg, who proclaimed the ending chaotic.

However, from the perspective of classical Hinduism, in continuing the saga beyond the earth, beyond heaven and hell to its conclusion in the otherworldly fourth domain, Vyāsa echoes the *Māṇḍukya Upaniṣad*'s fourfold analysis of reality. He reminds the listener that the life of bifurcated consciousness in the waking state is suffering. As long as human life is ensconced in individual selves it stands in opposition to the other. This opposition can lead to heaven or to hell. But the final scene, the last illusion, shows a return to unity. Here we find the happily-ever-after scene but with a twist. All the blemishes, all the marks have been removed. The bad guys are no longer bad, the good guys are no longer good. All such differentiations have been erased. The blind can now see, and the past has been forgotten in this festive communion. A yogic state of unity has been achieved; karma has been purged so that, in the words of Prajāpati in the *Chāndogya Upaniṣad*, "they arise from yonder space and reach the highest light, appear each with its own form...such a one is the supreme person. There such a one goes around laughing, sporting, having enjoyment with women or chariots or friends...all worlds and all desire have been appropriated by them."[7] There is only enjoyment, no strife, no separation, no other, only self. All have returned to their true self, and hence the action performed is pure illusion: not white, not black, not mixed.[8] The final scene is a metaphor for the ultimate *pralaya*, the *pralaya* of *nirvikalpa samādhi*, the state of utter pacification (*śānti*).[9] The emission of Vyāsa has returned to its source; the imaging and imagining has been played out. Without this conclusion, the story would be untrue to tradition, Zoroastrian at best. Here enemies truly disappear. Here consciousness without an object is made firm. Here also the audience concludes its austerity with *darśan*, a vision of pure silence, harmony, and bliss: no good, no bad, no struggle.

According to Vyāsa's tale, the struggle in life is not between good and evil: both share a common source. The struggle itself is the struggle and must be surrendered. Even the "good guys," despite their noble goals, are punished for violating dharma; the evil are rewarded for their resolve and steadfastness of purpose. The message here is one of transcending opposites: when we are in the game, the rules of the game must be applied. When the game is renounced, then final release is attained. And yet, we get the sense that for the fullness of life to be achieved the battle must take place. To be human is to desire, to bring forth worlds and ultimately lose those worlds. To live in these worlds is to suffer, and from our escape out of suffering, wisdom and freedom are attained.

Chapter 5

Nonviolent Approaches to Multiplicity

As seen in the previous chapter, one Hindu expression of nonviolence advocates seeing oneself as not different from others, an ethic similar to that found in the Golden Rule. For the Jaina tradition, the personal application of nonviolence extends to how one forms and holds opinions about others, fully acknowledging that differences exist in the world. If one assumes a posture of rigidity in defense of one's view, others may find this offensive. But if one holds no view of one's own, or has no sense of propriety, then one would be groundless, without purpose or identity, and presumably accepting of even violent actions. Both these extremes violate *ahiṃsā*. Rather than developing a form of absolutism or utter relativism, the Jaina outlook toward the ideas of others combines tolerance with a certainty in and commitment to Jaina cosmological and ethical views.

In this chapter we will discuss Jaina attitudes toward traditions that do not share their world view. Emphasis will be given to the sevenfold aspect of Jaina logic, and Jaina teachings about what are called "partial truths." This approach will be compared and contrasted with modern models for interreligious dialogue and Christian ecumenism. We will then examine some ways in which select Hindu texts such as the *Bhagavad Gītā* and the *Yoga Sūtra* cope with the issue of multiplicity, primarily through devices of structural accommodationism.

The fundamental teachings of Jainism state that the world is divided into nonliving and living components, that life forms have existed since beginningless time in myriad forms, and that life can be liberated through a fourteenfold process. These teachings have remained unchanged since their inception. In this regard, the Jaina tradition may be considered "fundamentalist" in the sense that its cosmology and ethics have not been subject to revision. Other historical issues have resulted in the emergence of two groups within the tradition, the Digambaras and Śvetāmbaras, but both exhibit a "remarkable unwillingness to depart from their basic doctrine and practices."[1] However, this fundamentalism is tempered by a fervent concern that the points of view held by others not be dismissed but rather that they be explored, understood, and then contextualized in the light of Jaina doctrine.

Much violence in the world has arisen due to fundamental religious disagreement. If persons with divergent cosmologies and ideologies can be given a framework through which to tolerate one another, nonviolence can prevail. With this in mind, the Jainas have exercised great care in articulating how their position differs from those of others, while not condemning alternate views as incorrect...only incomplete. This process requires that Jainas study the views of others, in order to more fully understand their own position.

The Jaina concern for understanding the traditions of others relative to their own is quite ancient. Record of it is found in the earliest texts of the Jaina canon. The *Sūtrakṛta*, included in the second section of Jaina canonical literature, critiques other systems of Indian thought in light of Jainism, specifically those that seem to advocate fatalism, eternalism, or vacuity. In the fifth century (C.E.), Siddhasena Divakaras' *Sanmatisūtra* investigates various viewpoints as being nonvalid when asserted in an absolutist manner. And in the thirteenth century, Mallisena's *Syādvādamañjari* offers a comprehensive critique of non-Jaina philosophical schools and religious practices.

The Jainas have shown great care to understand and respect the positions of others. They have been engaged in a form of dialogue with other traditions that has broadened their knowledge without altering their own faith commitment. Buddhists and Hindus also are known for referring to positions of others in order to clearly articulate their own views.[2] However, these traditions have also developed new forms that integrate and synthesize preexisting traditions. Hence, Māhayāna Buddhism appropriates Hindu deity forms; the Buddhist mind-only teaching is found in medieval Hindu texts; Ch'an Buddhism in China adopts the language of Taoism. Jainism, by contrast, did not develop substantially new forms, holding fast to its teachings on karma, *jīva*, and *ahiṃsā*.

The Jaina commitment to nonviolence arose out of a concern that action in the world promotes violence, violence results in additional karma and karma obstructs one from liberation. In addition to minimizing violence through vegetarianism, sweeping one's path, and covering one's mouth, the

Jainas also extended the nonviolent ethic to their logic as well. Rather than advancing a two-prong, wrong or right analysis of arguments in the style of Aristotle, and rather than stopping at the fourfold analysis of reality in the style of the Upaniṣads and Nāgārjuna,[3] the Jainas brought forth a sevenfold analysis of reality that specifically disallows the holding of any extreme view. Implicit in this approach is a recognition of the limitations imposed by linguistic structures and their ultimate irrelevance in light of the task and achievement of human liberation.

The seven views are outlined as follows:

1. In a certain way, a thing exists (*syād asti eva*)
2. In a certain way, a thing does not exist (*syād nāsti eva*)
3. In a certain way, a thing both exists and does not exist (sequentially) (*syād astyeva syānnāstyeveti*)
4. In a certain way, if existence and nonexistence are taken simultaneously, things are inexpressible (*syād avaktavyam*)
5. Hence, existent and inexpressible
6. Nonexistent and inexpressible
7. Existent, nonexistent, and inexpressible[4]

The first view acknowledges the existence of things within the world and speaks of the waking reality upon which we all presumably agree. The second view, familiar to students of Indian thought but not generally considered in Western analyses, reminds us that the very existence of a thing implies its nonexistence. This book was not here before it was written, nor will it endure eternally. The third view combines the first two, pointing out that things exist as moments within time but are subject to arising and decay. To speak of a thing purely in its existent phase as if it were eternal would be incorrect; to speak of things disparagingly because they are bound for destruction would represent an equally incorrect, nihilistic view. The fourth view points out that the true nature of a thing can never be expressed adequately; no matter how much I might want to say in order to describe someone dear to me, words fail to do more than denote particular and fragmentary aspects. Even to describe an apple becomes an impossibility. How can one speak of an apple without taking into account the tree from which it came, the person who planted the tree, the surface of the front of the apple, the surface (unseen) of the back of the apple, the nature of its interior, including its flesh, core, and seeds. "A rose by any other name is still a rose" becomes in the Jaina rendering "A rose has so many names it in fact is unspeakable." Consequently, once the paradox of ineffability is admitted, each of the earlier views is further qualified: existence is also unspeakable, nonexistence is unspeakable, and the joining of both is also unspeakable.

This logical construct makes all statements provisional. It is not skepticism in the strict sense of the word, but, in the words of H. R. Kapadia, it signifies that "every judgment that we pass in daily life is true only in reference to the standpoint occupied and the aspect of the object considered."[5] In the Jaina system, each truth is a partial one (*naya*) and no one statement (*anekāntavāda*) can ever account for the totality of reality. Kapadia relates this stance to the practice of nonviolence:

> When this *ahiṃsā* is allowed to play its role on an intellectual plane, it teaches us to examine and respect the opinions of others as they, too, are some of the angles of vision or pathways to reality which is many-sided and enable us to realize and practice truth in its entirety. This implies that ahiṃsā—the Jaina attitude of intellectual ahiṃsā—is the origin of anekāntavāda. In other words, the Jaina principle of 'respect for life'(ahiṃsā) is the origin of 'respect for the opinions of others' (anekāntavāda).[6]

For purposes of illustrating how the *syād-vāda* or perspectival method works, we will now examine a few key passages from the *Syādvādamañjari* of Mallisena, the thirteenth-century work mentioned earlier as an example of the Jaina concern for investigating the religious and philosophical positions of non-Jainas. This text analyzes the views of the Vaiśeṣika "atomists," the Nyāya logicians, the Pūrvamīmāṃsā ritualists, the Vedāntins, the adherents to the Sāṃkhya system, various schools of Buddhism, and the Lokāyata materialists. Mallisena's text is ostensibly written as a commentary on verses written by his teacher Hemacandra.

Sections IV through IX of the text critique the Vaiśeṣika system. The Vaiśeṣikas are criticized for being inconsistent, on the one hand asserting that a lamp is noneternal while on the other, that space is eternal. Within the Jaina system, as we have seen, no such inconsistency is allowed due to the teachings of atoms and space both being eternal. Mallisena then explains the Vaiśeṣika doctrine of a world-creating god, justified by his omnipresence, self-dependence, and eternity. The Jainas do not assent to the argument that a thing's presence proves that it has been created; the maker of a pot can be seen, so why is this creator-god invisible? If he is truly the author of scripture, then why would he praise himself therein? Why would he compose scriptures that contradict one another on the utility of animal sacrifice and the necessity of a

Brahman to have a son? The Jaina position considers the postulate of a creator god to be untenable logically and also states that such a notion weakens the perceived efficacy of karma.

The Nyāya logicians are criticized for their vagueness; the Pūrvamīmāṃsā school is criticized for its support of sacrificial animal slaughter. Vedānta's position on the nonduality of Brahman and the nonreality of the world is examined and then attacked on the grounds that if the world is not real, then how is it that the world is seen? "One is not both a mother and barren."[7] Sāṃkhya is criticized on four counts: its notion that consciousness can be devoid of object; that the *buddhi* (intellect) could be "nonintelligent," proclaiming that 'I am not'; that sky is born from the subtle element of sound; and that the witness (*puruṣa*) is neither bound nor liberated. From the Jaina perspective, each of these is contradictory.

Three distinct schools of Buddhism are presented. The Madhyāmika teachings on emptiness are dismissed as not adequately disproving the existence of either cogniser or cognition. The Sarvāstivādin doctrine of momentariness, wherein things come into existence, remain for a moment, go into decay, and then cease, is countermanded by the perdurability of memory. The Yogācāra technique of overcoming *vāsanā* (residues of karma), which emphasizes meditation, is deemed inadequate due to its being based on the doctrines of impermanence and no-self.

The final system critiqued by Mallisena is the Nāstikas or Nihilists who proclaim nothing has meaning or purpose. As a retort, the author notes that there is "purity of intelligence even on the part of one who has a body infected by leprosy,"[8] thus advancing an alternate, optimistic view of human potential.

In each of the instances mentioned above, Mallisena has clearly summarized the various schools examined. The critique he presents, while certainly not palatable from the perspective of those holding the respective views being discussed, holds true to Jainism's sevenfold analysis of reality and rejection of extreme views. Each system is acknowledged as a partial truth and hence validated, though not applauded.

The Jaina technique of rehearsing and then abrogating the "extreme" views of others illustrated above provides an interesting contrast with the *Yogavāsiṣtha*, a tenth or twelfth century syncretic Hindu text that explicitly integrates teachings of Buddhist momentariness with Vedāntin absolutism.[9] In both instances, it is made clear that India has long grappled with an issue that has come to the forefront in the West during the last thirty years: given the plurality of world religions that now come regularly into contact with one another, what hermeneutic approach is the most valid? Will the traditions more clearly define and maintain their integrity in light of their contact with other traditions? Will traditions begin to meld together, in the manner of late

Hinduism absorbing aspects of Buddhism, to the point where a discrete Buddhism disappeared?

The history of Christianity is replete with instances of both tendencies: inward-looking fundamentalism and outwardly influenced syncretism. On the one hand, the councils of Nicaea and Chalcedon were fundamentalist responses to movements within the Christian community that were considered suspect: Arianism, Monophysitism, Nestorianism, etc. The creeds aim to establish a clear, unambiguous definition as the foundation for Christian faith. And yet even the Gospels themselves are clearly the product of two cultural sensibilities joined together, the Hebrew and the Hellenistic. Likewise, as with Augustine and then with Aquinas, the insights of other cultures have shaped and reshaped the direction and orientation of Western Christianity. With Augustine we see an ascendance of personalistic, Neoplatonic, Manichaean religious forms; with Aquinas, thanks to the Islamic translations of Aristotle, we see yet another rewriting of the tradition. In each of these examples, the Christian faith seems less interested in maintaining fundamentals than in accommodating to new thought forms and issues.

Since the advent of rationalism, European colonialism, the rise of the academic study of world religion, and Vatican II, whole new revelations have been made accessible to the Christian world. As Thomas Berry has noted, the acknowledgement of and interest in world traditions potentially signals an infused vigor within the realm of theological discourse, unparalleled since the time of Thomas Aquinas. With this new development has arisen great debates over how best to proceed. In his recent book entitled *No Other Name? A Critical Survey of Christian Attitudes Toward the World Religions*, Paul Knitter offers a comprehensive survey of how various Christian denominations and thinkers have assessed this situation.[10] In some ways, this book, which describes itself as a textbook, is not unlike Mallisena's *Syādvādamañjari* and hence provides a similarly concise summary of a much larger body of literature. It surveys a host of positions, including the positions that all religions are relative (Troeltsch), that all are essentially the same (Toynbee), that all share a common psychic origin (Jung), that Christianity is the only true religion (Barth), that revelation is possible in other religions, while salvation is not (Tillich), that all religions are ways of salvation (Rahner). Knitter's own contribution attempts a new synthesis, building on the theocentric model of Hick, Panikkar, and Samartha.

Of the various models offered in Knitter's survey, the combined positions of Jung, Barth, and Tillich are closest to that of the Jainas. Like Jung, the Jainas see a commonality amongst *jīvas*: all hold the potential for liberation (though some lack the ability to achieve it). Like Barth, the Jainas are convinced of the sole effectiveness of their own tradition in achieving their goal. Like Tillich, they agree that partial truth is found elsewhere as well.

The solutions posed by Troeltsch, Toynbee, Rahner, and Knitter himself are more problematic from the Jaina perspective. Radical relativity would negate the efficacy of the Jaina system. Commonality of traditions (Toynbee) flies in the face of the perceived content of the respective traditions, as does the idea that all religions are ways of salvation (Rahner). Ultimately, however, the most troublesome of these viewpoints from a Jaina perspective would be that of theocentrism, which, in the eyes of the Jainas, would remove the religious process from human control; the Jainas refute the notion of any external divine force and assert that all religious experience come from one's own initiative.

In comparing the world view and method of contemporary ecumenists with that of the Jainas, there are both similarities and differences. Many ecumenists are searching for a unified truth, a basis for one's own belief that shares a ground of commonality with the religious life of others. For the Jainas, this quest for common ground does not exist. The Jainas are firm in their own belief structure: their cosmology, logic, and ethics have remained unaltered for nearly three thousand years and, as we have seen, Jainism clearly distinguishes itself from other traditions. In a sense, Jaina fundamentals are unshakable. However, accompanying this certitude is a driving concern to understand the beliefs of others, not to change themselves or even necessarily to convert others.

The work of contemporary Christian ecumenists, on the other hand, is often exploratory, creative, synthetic, and sometimes syncretic. However, this adventurousness carries with it the possibility of losing or altering one's own truths. As Seyyed Hossein Nasr has pointed out,

> Although based often on the positive intention of creating better understanding of other religions, most of the proponents of ecumenism place mutual understanding above the total integrity of a tradition to the extent that there are now those Christian theologians who claim that Christians should stop believing in the incarnation in order to understand Muslims and have Muslims understand them. One could only ask why they should remain Christians and not embrace Islam altogether.[11]

This is the inevitable conundrum of holding a logical system that seeks truth in monolithic terms. Nasr himself clearly and self-admittedly operates out of a commitment to esoteric experience that assents to the Vedāntic and Islamic vision of oneness; in his perspective, all religions are seen through this prism. However, like the Jainas (and unlike some ecumenists), Nasr defends holding strongly to one's own perspective while simultaneously advocating the exploration of other expressions of truth:

> The criticism that can be made against the religious exclusivists is not that they have strong faith in their religion. They possess faith but they lack principial knowledge, that kind of knowledge which can penetrate into foreign universes of form and bring out their inner meanings.[12]

In this instance, a more sympathetic eye is cast on the foundations of other traditions than has been evidenced by the Jainas.

Another approach, similar to the quest for commonality, has been suggested by Leonard Swidler. Unlike Nasr's emphasis on the divine or sacred as fundamental, Swidler offers an architectonic, "universal theology" that, as its ethos, allows "full human life" and "ultimate meaning."[13] However, just as Nasr's solution may sound odd to the nontheistic ears of a Jaina, so Swidler's appeal to a higher humanism might offend a Muslim because of its avoidance of God-language.

In this brief survey of interreligious encounters, three potential outcomes can be discerned: conversion, accommodationist syncretism, often in the form of a superinclusivistic metatheology, and renewed or tolerant or flexible fundamentalism.

Conversion is one very real option: undoubtedly some ecumenists have been converted unconsciously or in spite of themselves and would protest such a label. As Ewert Cousins has commented, one of the greatest challenges facing Christians who have had a genuine experience of Islam is to be able to return to the Christian Trinitarian tradition: the monotheism of the Islamic faith is very compelling and convincing. The emphasis on interiority found within South and East Asian traditions has been very attractive and effective for many.

Accommodationist syncretism has been a longstanding practice throughout Asia, with the interpenetration of Taoism, Buddhism, and Confucianism in China, Korea, and Japan, and the successive religious adaptations made in India when the Śramaṇic and Vedic traditions merged, when Śaṅkara infused Hinduism with Buddhism, when Guru Nanak brought Islam and Hindu ideas together, when Akbar formulated and instituted his Divine Wisdom religion, when Ram Mohan Roy began to integrate the Christian gospels with all of the above, and when Swami Vivekananda brought neo-Vedānta to the World Parliament of Religions in Chicago in 1893. Within the last decade, the New Age movement has introduced shamanic techniques into this melange. One difficulty with a "tradition" of this sort (and this is meant to also include inclusive ideologies such as benevolent humanism), is that the rigorous study and logical consistency that characterizes the "great traditions" becomes tenuous, though, as Raimundo Panikkar has pointed out, these matters should not be the litmus test for spiritual experience: "a rationality does not exhaustively define the human being."[14]

Renewed or tolerant or flexible fundamentalism, preferred by the Jainas, allows and in fact requires that the religiously informed person be well acquainted with how different traditions have approached the basic issues of human limitation and transcendence. It encourages respect for others' perspectives and yet allows one's primary commitment to remain rooted in that with which one feels most authenticated. It combines both perspectivalism and apologetics, as advocated by Paul Griffiths.[15]

There are several merits to the Jaina partial-truth view. The attack on religion by science as perceived by Creationists would be mitigated if we/they had access to a grammar that would allow us to say—"from a certain perspective, the world appears to be very ancient, and to have included many life forms. However, from the perspective of human suffering, this story can be read another way." This method allows various scenarios to possibly be the case, but does not deny or relativize the validity of one's own position. It also allows traditions and persons to discover commonalities without heralding those commonalities as absolutes. For instance, in regard to ethics, some aspects of liberation theology may be agreed upon by diverse faiths. The World Wildlife Fund has brought together religious leaders and scholars from various faiths to conceptually deal with the pressing problem of environmental decay. The solutions may proceed from diverse ideologies, perhaps often nonreligious ones, yet there need be no assumption that the ideologies themselves need to be changed. A respect for the viewpoint of others and a willingness to accept its contribution is made possible through the Jaina precept of *syād vāda*, that in a certain way and in a certain context, seemingly opposed or contradictory positions have value.

Fundamentalism is often viewed disparagingly as a blind devotion to a fixed set of beliefs to the point of excluding all other views. However, in order for a religious tradition to perform effectively, certain world views need to be agreed upon by its adherents; understandably these at times come into conflict. The Jaina solution to this dilemma is found in a logical structure that allows for and respects myriad positions yet holds to its own cosmological and ethical view. Jaina belief and precepts have not changed in over two and a half millenia, and yet Jainism survives with vigor in modern, industrial India. As various forms of Christianity, Buddhism, Hinduism, and Islam enter into dialogue with their own multiple forms and with one another, new structures are needed to identify what beliefs are essential and central to one's own subtradition and tradition and how these may best be articulated and then related to the traditions of others. The Jaina model of flexible fundamentalism offers one option for validating a fundamentalist devotion to basic teachings while still acknowledging the validity of divergent views within their own context.

The Hindu approach to multiplicity has been referred to as inclusivist.[16] However, the term inclusivist might seem to indicate that the variant positions included are part of an overarching schematic, or answerable to some sort of central deity or monistic absolute. To the contrary, if we examine some of the many ideas included in what some characterize as Hinduism, there seems to be no such possible absolute. Even the *Bhagavad Gītā*, often called the Hindu Bible, contains divergent perspectives and has been used to support a host of positions, only some of which can be said to include others. Just as Krishna presented many perspectives to Arjuna, so have many scholars, both traditional and modern, held many perspectives on the *Bhagavad Gītā*. Robert N. Minor, whose own position is that the "the Gita proclaims as its hightest message the lordship of Kṛṣṇa and the highest response of the human being to that lordship is devotion, *bhakti*,"[17] notes several different usages of the text by different theologians. For Śaṅkara (788–820 C.E.), the message is the "end of the world and its accompanying activity." Madhusudana and Venkatanātha, while not rejecting Śaṅkara's view, place more emphasis on devotion, as does Jñāneśvara, the Marathi commentator. Bhaskara takes issue with Śaṅkara's interpretation, asserting that the world is a real aspect of Brahman. Rāmānuja used the *Gītā* in support of his position that "the true self is not divine and not one with the other selves, though in liberation is identical in knowledge to those other selves." Nimbarka, a twelfth-century thinker, prompted interpretations that see Krishna as teaching "innate nonidentity in identity." Madhva (1238–1317), the famous dualist, "radically reinterprets the text so that it asserts an eternal and complete distinction between the Supreme, the many souls, and matter and its divisions." Minor also cites modern interpretations by Bal Gangadhar Tilak and Mohandas K. Gandhi, who used the text to help inspire the independence movement, and Sri Aurobindo, Sarvepalli Radhakrishnan, and Swami Vivekananda, who took a syncretic approach to the text.[18]

Few of the scholars cited above seem to agree on the meaning of the text, yet none of them can be said to be incorrect. It may be argued that this utter contextualization of the text causes it to fall into a fatal relativism; that the text, because it is open to so many interpretations and has been used to confirm opposing positions ranging from Śaṅkara's monism to Madhva's dualism, is trivial and perhaps meaningless. But how, then, could such a text survive? How can one account for or even describe a text that includes and is used to support a virtual cacophony of traditions and positions? Setting aside even the interpretations of later commentators mentioned above, how can the explicitly nontheistic Sāṃkhya appear alongside the thoroughly theistic *bhakti* approach also taught by Krishna?

Max Mueller addressed a similar issue when trying to cope with the multiplicity of gods in the *Ṛg Veda* and invented a term to describe it:

> To identify Indra, Agni, and Varuna is one thing, it is syncretism; to address either Indra or Agni or Varuṇa, as for the time being the only god in existence with an entire forgetfulness of all other gods, is quite another; it was this phase, so fully developed in the hymns of the *Veda* which I wished to mark definitely by a name of its own, calling it henotheism.[19]

The Vedic method that extols different gods within the same text is similar to that employed in the *Bhagavad Gītā*, in which each time Arjuna asks Krishna for one truth, again and again Krishna offers Arjuna yet another perspective, another chapter, another yoga. Each view, whether that of a god being sacrificed to or a yogic discipline being practiced, is given life as long as it proves effective. Multiplicity is the rule, with one god, one perspective gaining and holding ascendancy as long as it, he, or she proves efficacious. That one is then swept from its elevated position as new situations and new questions emerge; yet, if pressed, a Hindu will always admit, of course, Indra is best; of course, Agni is best; of course, Varuṇa is best; of course, Karma Yoga is best, of course, Bhakti Yoga is best.

Antonio T. deNicolás has explained this phenomenon philosophically as

> a systematic and methodic effort to save rationality in its plural manifestations through an activity of embodiment that emancipates man from any form of identification, allowing him the freedom to act efficiently in any one identifiable field in the social fabric.[20]

Just as the many gods of the Vedas are effective in different situations, so the many yogas are prescribed in the *Gītā* without compromising or subordinating one to another. Mutual paths are allowed to exist in complementarity.

In a sense, the *Gītā* is composed in the spirit of the Jaina approach to truth. The Jainas assert that every statement is an utterance of partial truth; all postulation is rendered senseless by the ultimate postulate that no words are ever totally adequate to describe experience (*avaktavya eva*). Similarly, Krishna painstakingly guides Arjuna through many yogas, yet the entire problem is obliterated when Krishna reveals his true form to Arjuna. All the words, all the individual personalities and collective armies are swallowed up by the gaping mouth of Krishna, the origin and dissolution of all things. The net result is that all possibilities are present for Arjuna when he gains the knowledge that all are impermanent.

The *Bhagavad Gītā* sets forth a multiplicity of possible paths. A panoply of perspectives is offered to the reader in a nonjudgmental way; the many positions proposed by Krishna do not necessarily compete with one another but rather complete one another. If one needs to act, one uses Karma Yoga; if one needs to meditate, one uses Dhyāna Yoga. This "henocretic" text is written with a gentle tolerance, allowing various practices and positons to be pursued, but, unlike Jainism, without insisting upon a unified or even consistent view.

Similarly, the *Yoga Sūtra* of Patañjali (ca. 100 C.E.), which combines practices such as nonviolence from the Jaina tradition and the *Brahmavihāra* from the Buddhist tradition, copes with multiplicity in a pragmatic fashion. Focusing primarily on practices that lead to a state of spiritual insight, it describes both the path and the goal pluralistically.

The *Yoga Sūtra* consists of a concatenation of distinct schools of yoga, which can be variously designated as *nirodha yoga, samādhi yoga, kriyā yoga, aṣṭāṅga yoga,* along with practices drawn from the Buddhists, Jainas, and perhaps others. However, I hesitate to describe Patañjali's process with the term syncretism, defined by Berling as "borrowing, affirmation, or integration of concepts, symbols or practices of one religious tradition into another by a process of selection and reconciliation."[21] Patañjali simply does not reconcile or mathematically "total out" the diverse practices he mentions; as Frauwallner has written, "The *Yoga Sūtra* of Patañjali is composed of different constituents or elements which, in no way, give a uniform homogenous picture."[22] However, the text has been immensely successful, surviving nearly two millenia.

Contradictions are seemingly present in the *Yoga Sūtra* of Patañjali; it undoubtedly would not withstand the consistency test of modern analytic philosophers. However, the method used by Patañjali seems to reflect some of the central concerns of the system itself. Various paths are announced, but judgments are not pronounced; no teaching is said to be higher or better. Differences between the various systems of practice are not denied, nor are they even discussed. The method by which Patañjali presents the various yogas is consistent with their goal as if having himself become established in *kaivalyam*, he surveys them with a dispassionate eye, seeing the possibility of each. His techniques coexist as complements, not as competitors.

In both the multiperspectival tolerance of the Jainas and the accommodationist juxtapositions of the Hindus, models of understanding are offered that allow one to account for and to respect the other without denying, contradicting, or converting. The most violent acts arise from the nonacceptance of another's viewpoint. The inability to expand or alter one's own opinions often brings about the objectification of those who do not cleave to that particular vision. Herein lies the challenge and subtle profundity of the *ahiṃsā* doctrine. When pursued with diligence it leads to a world view that calls into question the very premises of self and the relationship of self with the objective world. How can something be possessed if that which one yearns to possess is in essence the same as oneself? How can a point of view be derided if in fact the holder of that point of view is not different from oneself? Intellectual nonviolence requires a commitment to one's own belief system accompanied with an ability to tolerate and perhaps even celebrate the positions of others.

Chapter 6

The Jaina Path of Nonresistant Death

Fasting comprises an important part of Jaina religious life, for both laypersons and members of monastic orders. By abstaining from food for one or more days, Jainas claim that one purges various forms of negative karma. The most frequent fast is the *poṣadhapavāsa*, which requires fasting on the "eighth and fourteenth days of the moon's waxing and waning periods."[1] By not eating, one renounces harm to the *jīvas* present in the food that normally would be consumed, thereby expelling previous karma and preventing the accrual of new karma. In this chapter we will examine the ultimate fast upon which many Jainas embark: the *sallekhanā* or fast unto death, considered to be the most auspicious way that life can end.

The *Ācārāṅga Sūtra*, a primary text of the Jaina tradition, states that all beings desire to live. This includes oneself, and some violence is necessary to survive; eating necessarily involves the taking of life, even if vegetable. The hierarchical life forms seemingly prioritize which offenses against life are most serious and prescribe how best to minimize violence. However, when it is clear that one's life will be over soon, Jainas are encouraged to accept their imminent death and in fact actively embrace it through engaging in a final fast, facilitating their own demise in such a way that no further violence is fostered.

The act of taking one's life has many forms in the history and traditions of India.[2] As Yajneshwar S. Shastri has noted, several forms of voluntary death are attested to in Hinduism, Jainism, and Buddhism: *mahāprasthāna*, the great journey such as that undertaken by the five Pāṇḍava brothers and their wife

Draupadī at the end of the *Mahābhārata; jalasamādhi,* drowning in a sacred river; *agnipraveśa,* entering into fire, the most familiar form of this being *sati* or the immolation of widows; *bhṛgupatana,* jumping off a cliff (in the *Tīrthavivecanakanda* of Kṛtyakalpataru it is stated that persons who jump from Mount Amarakantaka never are born again); *jauhar,* self-destruction to prevent capture and exploitation by an enemy, in the style of Masada, where a community of Jews committed mass suicide rather than submit to the Romans; offering one's flesh to birds of prey or wild animals, the most famous example being from the Jātaka tales in which in a prior incarnation the future Buddha offers his own flesh to a lioness so that she may feed her starving cubs; and *prāyopaveśana,* fasting unto death, referred to in the Jaina tradition as *sallekhanā.*[3]

If death is self-inflicted for any cause other than religious piety or social justice, it is deemed suicide (*ātmaghāta* or *ātmahanana*) in Indian tradition and soundly condemned. Not only are such persons guaranteed rebirth in hell or as demons, but various texts tell of abuses heaped upon the bodies of successful suicides: Kautilya's *Arthaśāstra* states that no funeral rituals may be performed for suicides and that the dead body is to be exposed along a public roadway.[4] Such acts of self-destruction would be associated with self-indulgence and despair, undertaken due to hopelessness rather than commitment to a higher goal, whether this-worldly or other-worldly. The saint Pujyapada made the distinction between ritual death and suicide by explaining that "*samādhi* death is devoid of attachment (*rāga*) while suicide is motivated and accompanied by passion."[5]

In Western culture, with the exception of the Masada incident mentioned above, self-immolation for any purpose is not generally deemed acceptable. Even the occurrence at Masada is debated amongst rabbinical scholars, some of whom find the action taken there to be extreme: life is too sacred to be violated through intervention of one's own will. The mass suicide in Jonestown, Guyana, was perhaps undertaken in imitation of this precedent, though none can deny that the entire affair was fundamentally misguided. Other incidents of conscious self-immolation for a higher cause in recent memory are the Irish nationalists who fasted to death in protest of British policies, and the pacifists who set fire to themselves demonstrating against the war in Vietnam, including Norman Morrison, a Quaker from Baltimore, who set himself on fire on the steps of the Pentagon on November 2, 1965.

Fasting in India has been used as a political tool. In one particular type (*prayā* in Sanskrit, *dharna* in Hindi), Brahmins undergo public fasting in an attempt to change policy. In the Indian historical records on this practice, this "fasting against" was often answered with a counterfast by the King; whoever ended the fast first lost the dispute.[6] Gandhi employed this sort of fast with success; the Irish nationalists have not been so fortunate.

Fasting unto death in the Jaina tradition is undertaken only if very specific criteria are met. As Colette Caillat has noted, "Before it can be resorted to, all worldly ties are to be severed: the individual will already be out of this world; and...should be pure in all respects."[7] In Samantabhadra's *Ratnakaraṇḍaka Śrāvakācāra*, a text of the second century of the common era, it is stated that such a fast is acceptable only in four situations: calamity, severe famine, old age, or illness from which there is no escape or against which there is no remedy.[8] This text goes on to state that

> one should give up gradually all solid foods, increase the taking of liquids like milk, then give up even liquids gradually and take warm water. Thereafter, one should give up warm water also, observe the fast to the best of one's ability with determination and depart from the body repeating the *namaskāra mantra* continuously till the last. During the observance of the vow, one should not commit any of the transgressions: entertaining a desire to live, wishing for a speedy death, exhibiting fear, or desire to meet friends or remembering them or expecting to be born with all comforts and pleasure in the next life.[9]

In the *Puruṣārthasiddhyupāya*, a twelfth-century text written by Amṛtacandra, the following verses address the issue of the final fast:

> 89. One should not kill himself by zealously giving one's own flesh as food to another starving person, seen approaching in front.
>
> 175. One should ever be devotedly thinking of Sallekhana at the end, that "it is only this which would enable me to carry my wealth of piety with me."
>
> 176. "I shall certainly observe Sallekhana properly at the approach of death," is the thought one should constantly have and thus be practicing the vow prematurely.
>
> 177. On account of the absence of any emotion, there is no suicide by one acting in this manner, on the certain approach of death, because of the observance of Sallekhena, the passions are attentuated.
>
> 178. He who, actuated by passion, puts an end to life by stopping breath, or by water, fire, poison, or weapons, is certainly guilty of suicide.

> 179. In the practice of Sallekhana, all passions, which cause Himsa, are subdued, and hence Sallekhana is said to lead to *Ahiṃsā.*[10]

In these passages, it is clear that *sallekhanā* is distinguised from suicide, which is condemned even if for the sake of allowing a starving person to live. *Sallekhanā* is seen as the ultimate practice of nonviolence, preparing one for clear passage into the death state and beyond.

For the Jainas, it is regarded as an act of spiritual purification, a *tapas* that strengthens a person as she or he prepares to enter into death. By fasting at or near or toward the point of death, the distractions of digestion and desire for food are eliminated, allowing purified concentration as preparation for the transitional moment. Caillat has noted:

> It is natural that a creed which believes in the saving power of tapas should endeavour to derive benefit from it, especially at crucial instants, when death is drawing near. The Jainas, therefore, like many other Indians, try to determine the conditions which, for one preparing for "death in perfect conditions" (*samādhi-maraṇa*), will lead to good rebirth, or, even, to "perfection" (*siddhi*), ie. deliverance (*mukti*), sometimes also called *nirvāṇa.*[11]

The purification of karma that results from fasting enables one to either advance to a better life after death, or obtain final release.

Various instances of the fast unto death are found in the canon of the Śvetāmbara sect, most of which are modeled on the spiritual career of Khandaga Kaccayana, a disciple of Mahāvīra who led an exemplary life as a Jaina monk; his spiritual accomplishments are indicated by the observation that he was "piled high with mortification (*tapas*) and piled low with flesh and blood, and like a fire confined within a heap of ashes he shone mightily with glow (*tapas*), with lustre (*tejas*) and with the splendour of glowing lustre."[12] At the end of his days, after twelve years as a wandering monk, he is granted permission by Mahāvīra to enter into the final fast, whereupon he climbed Mount Vipula and sat "with his face to the east, the ten fingers of his hands clasped before his forehead with joined palms, and recited the appropriate [*mantras*]."[13] Following the death of Khandaga, Mahāvīra states that he will be reborn as a god in one of the highest heavens, after which he will achieve final liberation (*parinirvāṇa*).

Throughout the state of Karnataka in south India, particularly in the area surrounding Śravanabelgola, several ancient inscriptions attest to the extensive practice of the *sallekhanā* fast. A few of the many examples given in R. Narasimhachar's *Inscriptions at Śravanabelgola* are cited as follows:

> Ācārya Ariṣṭanemi was a great Ācārya who had come to the south with many disciples. He was received by queen Kaṃpita and the king Kindikā [and]...went up the Kaṭavapra hill....he gave up his food and became engrossed in pure meditation on the self and attained perfection....
>
> Nāgamati appears to have been a nun and she expired after observing the vow for three months....
>
> A holy nun by name Jambu Nāyagir expired after observing the vow for a period of one month....
>
> Baladeva Guru was the disciple of Dharmasena Guru. He expired after keeping the vow of saṃnyāsana for one month....
>
> Sasimati was a nun; she was possessed of noble qualities and had performed many devotional acts. She had studied the scriptures extensively. She came to Raḷvappu and saw that her end was near. She thought to herself: "This is the course I have to adopt." She ascended the holy hill and observed the vow....[14]

Two notables who exemplified the decision to fast unto death, also from Śravanabelgola, are Mallisena Maladharideva, a monk, and a laywoman, Macikabbe. According to Shadakshari Settar, of Karnatak University,

> Exalted by his supreme renunciation and meditation, he [Mallisena] abandoned his perishable body as if to fully destroy Cupid, the dominator of the mortal frame. His mind, a bee at the divine lotus-feet of the illustrious Ajitasena-panditadeva, he prepared himself to abandon his body according to the rite of *sallekhanā* celebrated in the *Jinagamas.* Without exhibiting any signs of exhaustion, he composed [a devotional] verse on his deathbed, as if to testify to the ripeness of his mind, and sang it to the raptures of the whole congregation of devotees and disciples who had assembled to witness the rite of *samādhi*....
>
> ...Thus, after gaining the *ratna-trayas* [three jewels of Jaina faith], and seeking the blessings of the Jina, he saved himself from causing pain to any living being. Observing the fast for three days, he ended his life on Sunday, 10th March, 1129 A.D..[15]

Macikabbe, a widow whose heart was finally broken by the death of her daughter, decided that to continue living was futile:

> Being the "horn of plenty" (the all-giving "celestial cow") to her dependents, she asked "who wants what?," and liberally distrib-

> uted all that she possessed. Having gifted away everything, she took leave of her relatives with dignity, and departed to Belgola.
>
> Taking the severe vow of *saṃyāsana* in the presence of her *gurus* Prabhacandra Siddhantadeva, Ravicandra and Vardhamanadeva, she enriched her mind with spiritual knowledge and prepared herself to complete the difficult task. Adopting a posture of half-closed eyes, she set her mind on the lotus-feet of Lord Jina and repeatedly chanted the five expressions (*pañcapadas*). Fasting for one month, embracing the *saṇyāsa*, listening to the account of the *samādhi*, narrated by her teacher and other saints she effortlessly attained the state of gods, amidst the plaudits of earth-dwellers.[16]

In total, eighty epitaphs from Karnataka sites as translated by Narasimhachar document death by fasting, spanning a period from about 600 to 1809.[17]

European observers have commented on this practice. Mrs. Sinclair Stevenson, noted for her thorough though slanted description of the Jaina tradition published in 1915, comments that

> The influence of a negative religion is then worked out to its irresistible conclusion, and with all the sorrows and ills of the world awaiting to be relieved, the soldier deserts his post in order to free his own soul from suffering. It is strange that a religious system which begins with the most minute regulations against the taking of the lowest insect life should end by encouraging human suicide.[18]

In a slightly more positive vein, Louis Renou, having seen persons during the fasting process, seemingly acknowledges and respects the religious import of the practice:

> It is not unusual to see one of them (as I have) freely choose to die in the way characteristic of the Jainas, ending a life of austerities by abstaining from food altogether. Nevertheless, it is a way of death that many aspire after eagerly; postulants beseech the Master to admit them to it; relations and friends add their entreaties on the applicant's behalf.[19]

His description indicates the gravity with which the *sallekhanā* fast is entered into, as well as the highly venerated status which it is accorded.

While visiting Jaina Vishva Bharati in Ladnun, Rajasthan, in December, 1989, I had the opportunity of being present during the fast unto death of an infirm eighty-year-old nun of the Terapanthi Śvetāmbara sect of Jainism. A group of novice nuns in the campus convent hall informed me that a woman named Sadhvi Kesharji had taken the vow to fast unto death (*santhara* or *sallekhanā*) twenty-eight days prior, and that I would be allowed to see her while Acharya Tulsi, the leader of the Terapanthi order, met with her. The nuns escorted me quickly downstairs and, in a medium-sized room, the three top Terapanthi leaders were arrayed in front of this tiny octogenarian nun. Acharya Tulsi invited me to sit next to him directly in front of her as he spoke with her and blessed her. He pointed out that she had a great deal of courage and was able to do this because she had no desire for life or death. He emphasized her bravery. He blessed her with the Mangalacarya chant and spoke of the momentousness of the occasion and the locale. The building, designed to house four hundred nuns during their periodic study times at the university, was newly built, and this was the first such fast conducted on the premises. The nun replied by stating that she had waited until he (Acharya Tulsi) could be there to declare the fast; most often nuns or *munis* (monks) die when they are on the road, and pass on without the benefit of seeing their preceptor. She expressed gratitude and happiness at seeing him clearly. Acharya Tulsi commented how cheerful her faced looked, and stated that this was a joyous event. He also said this was very unlike a Western-style death or a death where life is prolonged by "injections and technology." I was told by my host, S. L. Gandhi, that the nun had undergone one surgery and that another would have been required. The nun had decided to undertake the fast rather than prolong her life, though she certainly had fulfilled the Jaina requirement that the fast not be entered into until death is imminent. The woman's daughter, also a Jaina nun, was by her side and in fact helped her to sit up; her physician was also present. Ultimately, her fast lasted for forty days.

Later in the day, during an audience with Acharya Tulsi, I inquired regarding the spiritual status of the fasting nun. One of the novice nuns had earlier told me that the older woman was entering into a state of *nirvāṇa* by virtue of her fast; this would be the fourteenth or final *guṇasthāna*. However, Acharya Tulsi corrected this perception, saying that all karmas are eliminated in the final stage and that the nun, by virtue of her vows, had reached only the sixth or seventh stage. He also said that the highest state possible for laypersons is the fifth stage, accessible to persons who have had *samyak dṛṣṭi* and take the twelve basic vows of the layperson.[20] He also said that monks or laypersons can fall as low as the first *guṇasthāna* of ignorance (*mithyādṛṣṭi*). Interestingly, a layman seated next to me quickly spoke up and stated that by the time of her actual death she could dispel all her karmas and reach the fourteenth stage. The Acharya did not agree or disagree with this statement. In a later discussion, a lay group fervently discussed this issue and asserted that from their perspective laypersons can also reach the final state, citing as their authority the *Ācārāṅga Sūtra*, which according to them states that one's uniform, whether monastic or lay, does not determine one's spiritual evolution. These various encounters underscored the independence of opinion that is so greatly cherished in the Jaina tradition of multidimensionality (*anekāntavāda*).

My first awareness of the sallekhanā tradition came via the opening passage of Padmanabh S. Jaini's *The Jaina Path of Purification*, where the fasting to death of Śāntisāgara in 1955 is described. My impression from this description was that this event happens only very rarely (this description being published twenty-four years after the fact) and that the ritual fast could only be pursued by the highest of the spiritual elite (Śāntisāgara was head of the Digambara Jaina community). However, while in Madras the next week, I learned that the fast unto to death is not limited in modern practice to monks and nuns; a prominent member of the Jaina community there told me that his own octogenarian father, having been diagnosed as terminally ill, took a fast unto death and after twenty-eight days passed away, the day after he saw one of his lifelong projects brought to completion.[21]

In both of these instances, as well as in the historical cases mentioned earlier, entering into the fast unto death is restricted to a small number of religiously devout Jainas. It springs from a vision of life and the life process that sees no finality in death; life, according to Jaina doctrine, cannot be killed but transforms into a new form. Even the final goal of liberation or kevala is not seen as death but rather as a final detachment from involvement in the things of the world: the *jīva* lives on eternally, with untrammeled energy, consciousness, and bliss. The vow of nonviolence, and its accompanying supports, is said to diminish the karmas that prevent one from achieving this highest state. The final vow accelerates this process by honing down even hunger, the most basic of human and hence karmic desires.

In dealing with ethical virtues, we systematically confront a number of cultural presuppositions that prescind from an agreed-upon cosmological view. In the American context we have inherited a variety of ideas and responses regarding the topic of death. On the one hand there is an eschatological approach to death; death is seen as a finality. From our residual and collective religious explanations of the death experience, it is heard that death leads either to a state of blessedness or damnation depending upon one's deeds, a state that can only be altered with the ultimate eschatological event of the Messiah's return at the end of history. From another and perhaps more modernist perspective, death is faced with dread and fear. Even for those moderns to whom heaven and hell have been disproven by science, there is still an abiding assessment that life is somehow good and that death, in the terror of its unknowability, lurks around the corner as the ultimate unseen evil.

In either case, religious or secular, death is a feared finality, usually to be postponsed at all costs. Ernest Becker in his *Denial of Death* and Elizabeth Kübler-Ross in *On Death and Dying*, along with many others, have pointed out that Western cultural resources for dealing with death are fraught with fear, avoidance, and denial. Without attempting too facile an analysis, perhaps it can be conjectured that the value placed on the immediacy and importance of this one life stems from both the prophetic Judeo-Christo-Islamic eschatological world view that values the uniqueness of both the human soul and its personalistic experience and the natural law world view that assesses the human person in terms of inalienable rights to pursue happiness and liberty. In the former, death is seen as a gateway to eternal life; in the latter, the immediacy of the moment takes precedence over theories regarding an afterlife.

In Indian traditions, we are often reminded of death in the stories of the *Mahābhārata*, and elsewhere. Gāṅgā, the beautiful and mysterious wife of Śantanu, the progenitor of the Kuru clan, is depicted drowning her own infant children year after year. When queried regarding her strange behavior after several have been born, she replies that she is merely returning the babies to their source and thereby sparing them the suffering unavoidable when one takes human birth. Death often appears as the god Yama in Indian stories and numerous goddesses in the Hindu tradition, including Kālī and Sitalā, are notable for their association with death. In these guises, death takes on a familiarity unknown in the Western world other than his depiction as the grim reaper.

For the Jainas, death is seen as an opportunity to redeem the residues of past action and enter clearly into a new embodiment. As noted earlier, the concept of each *jīva*'s immortality dismisses out of hand the notion that death is anything other than transitional. Life and death alike involve the reconfiguration of the *jīva*, based on the balance of karmic influx and purgation. The goal of religious practice is to disperse karma, thus guaranteeing a purified life in the present, a better future life, and ultimately a religious life, signaling the first step toward total liberation. The vows of Jainism challenge the limits of human capability: to assiduously avoid the taking of life requires immense concentration and devotion. For approved persons, the various vows taken to alter one's lifestyle in accord with *ahiṃsā* may be seen merely as preliminary to taking on the final vow when death grows near. Though clearly (and exclusively) for the most earnest devotees of the Jaina faith, it, like the other Jaina vows, prompts reflection on one's own attitudes toward the sanctity of life and death.

The Jaina vows of vegetarianism and restricted travel helped change the face of Hinduism. Jaina teachings on nonviolence helped inspire Mahatma Gandhi and Martin Luther King, Jr., to work at overthrowing injustice. The vow of *sallekhanā*, when properly understood as being other than suicide, presents an interesting counterpoint to some of the current discussion of medical ethics, specifically in the realm of euthanasia. Though it clearly exhibits a position distinct from that of the Hemlock Society, in which the pursuit of death is aggressive, the Jaina community would seemingly be supportive of a noninterventionist approach on issues of prolonging life. Depending on the spiritual mettle of the affected person, the use of life-support systems would probably be rejected if the person were ready and eager to face death (as clearly has been demonstrated as a possibility in the Jaina tradition) or if the person were unable to make a choice. As with all aspects of Jainism, the consent and desire of the person would be essential, a life that would view death not as a finality but as part of an ongoing, inalienable continuity.

In the area of Christian moral theology, suicide and euthanasia are both generally regarded to be morally unacceptable.[22] However, none can deny that some of the techniques now available to prolong life border on the inhuman; John Paul II states that care must be taken in "judging whether the expense and personnel is disproportionate to the forseeable results and whether the medical techniques used will cause the sick person suffering or inconvenience greater than the benefits that may be derived from them."[23] In certain cases, it is deemed acceptable to discontinue use of life-support systems. However, the case of the *sallekhanā* fast would not be an entertainable notion in most sects of the Christian tradition, any more so than the type of suicide advocated by the Hemlock Society. In the words of Gerald Kelly, S.J., "God is the creator and master of human life and no one may take it without His authorization."[24] The Jaina world view differs radically from the Christian: it has no creator god and asserts through its doctrines of *jīva* and karma that persons are solely responsible for their own destiny. Consequently, grounds for dialogue on the issue of death and dying would most likely be limited to the psychological arena, wherein the bravery and freedom from fearfulness exhibited by Jaina *sallekhanā* practitioners can be seen as an inspiring alternative to the fear and loathing associated with death in Western traditions.

The nonviolent self in this instance is embodied in the person who no longer holds firmly to the notion that his or her individual biography has ultimacy. In a certain sense, the monastic life lived by the Jainas is a form of living death, but not in a macabre sense. The simplicity of lifestyle, stemming from a commitment to nonviolence, strips away nonessentials and reveals the core of a living, breathing, occasionally food-consuming being not driven by conventionality or desire. Such a being can freely enter death with less clutter and concern, paving the way for either a similarly purified life or perhaps even total release. The integrity and clarity of this way of life and death can speak deeply to the condition of those nearing death or near the death of another. In the words of the *Bhagavad Gītā*, where Krishna advises Arjuna on the proper attitude that he must cultivate in regard to death:

> Unmanifest are all beings in their beginning, O Bharata, manifest in their middle states, and unmanifest again in their ends. What is there to lament?[25]

By maintaining the perspective that all things born must die but in fact will be born again or born into a state of perpetual energy, consciousness, and bliss, the Jaina tradition offers a view of life that offers not hope but a sense of equanimity and acceptance. According to the structures of karma, the energies of past deeds are not utterly dissipated with the demise of the body, but will continue, whether they foster goodness, evil, or the blessedness of release. Through the practice of nonviolence, both evil and inhibiting attachment to goodness are overcome, paving the way for release.

Chapter 7

Living Nonviolence

We have examined the spread of nonviolence or *ahiṃsā* from its possible early origins in India, and have explored its centrality to Jainism. We have discussed briefly its influence on Hinduism and its movement with Buddhism into China and Japan. We also have considered its continued relevance in light of contemporary physical and psychic needs. In many ways, the essential issues addressed by the *ahiṃsā* doctrine have not changed. For millenia, animals have been sacrificed in religious rituals; today animals continue to be sacrificed, but now in the name of science. The earth in past centuries was subjected to deforestation and erosion of soil; today the scope of such devastation threatens the existence of countless species, and the air and water are threatened as never before. Human conflict has long been a source of consternation, as evidenced by an undying legacy of religious strife and war. And death, though in modern times often postponed and sanitized, nonetheless persists to perplex and confound.

In this study we have surveyed the possible contributions that nonviolent theory and practice can make to each of these problems, exploring how traditional vows can be applied and extended to meet contemporary needs. Through vegetarianism and nonpossession, harm to animals and the earth can be reduced. Through the adoption of tolerant atitudes toward the views of others as modeled by the perspectival logic of the Jainas, religious conflict can be eased. The monistic teachings on nonviolence as found in the *Mahābhārata* likewise offer a method for deconstructing the objectification of the other that can so easily lead to discord. And the Jaina approach to death through a final fast, as shocking a it may seem, gives one pause to reconsider the ready use of technology to delay death that has become so prevalent in modern society.

Ahiṃsā emerges from a world view based on notions of karma that link violent activity to future painful retribution. This mechanistic model has found theoretical expression in diverse Jaina, Buddhist, and Hindu forms. The Jainas posit the existence of uncountable life forms (*jīvas*), each seeking liberation from the shackles of karma. The Buddhists practice noninjury to life due to the precept that all life is fleeting, that no self exists, that all things hence merit compassion. Various schools of Hinduism have stated that the Vedic ritual is ineffective; that it is far better to see the Self (*ātman*) in all beings than to perform even a hundred sacrifices. Each of these perpectives differs radically from one another, yet all these traditions, despite various explanations and justifications, remain rooted in nonviolence as their primary ethical virtue and all agree upon the efficacy of the law of karma.

Nonviolence and the Western World

A constructive theology of reverence for life based on nonviolent practices can accord well not only with the current effort to reverse environmental destruction and protect animal life, but also resonates with some values, both aesthetic and ethical, that are at the core of life and history in the Western world. Is this mere coincidence? Just as we have seen a thread of continuity in the spread of the nonviolent ethic from its home in India throughout the Buddhist world, some scholars have suggested that Indian renouncer traditions had a direct influence on Greek and later European thought.[1] In the *Geography* of Strabo (63 B.C.E.–21 C.E.), we find that the Mediterranean world was well acquainted with certain aspects of religion in India. Referring to Megasthenes (c. 350–290 B.C.E.), Strabo describes Alexander's contact with Indian ascetics, and distinguishes between two different forms of Indian religion, the Brahmanic or priestly and Śramaṇic (Garmanes), the renouncers. He writes that

> ...the philosophers tarry in a grove in front of the city in an enclosure merely commensurate with their needs, leading a frugal life, lying on straw mattresses and skins, abstaining from animal food and delights of love, and hearkening only to earnest words, and communicating also with anyone who wishes to hear them...they believe that the life here is, as it were, that of a babe still in the womb, and that death, to those who have devoted themselves to philosophy, is birth into the true life, that is, the happy life; and

> that they therefore discipline themselves most of all to be ready for death.[2]
>
> As for the Garmanes (Sramans), he says that the most honorable of them are named Hylobii (Forest Dwellers) and that they live in forests, subsisting on leaves and wild fruits, clothed with bark of trees, and abstaining from wine and the delights of love; and that they communicate with the kings, who through messengers inquire about the causes of things...[3]
>
> ...they stay in one posture all day long without moving... women, as well as men, study philosophy with some of them, and...the women likewise abstain from the delights of love.[4]

Strabo also describes conversations wherein the Indian renouncers praise as "soundminded" Pythagorean vegetarianism, and tells the story of Calanus, an Indian philosopher who traveled with Alexander the Great.

Clement of Alexandria, the Christian thinker who lived in the late second century C.E., using both Strabo and Alexander Polyhistor of the first century B.C. as references, condemns Indian religious practices in his *Stromateis:*

> There are some who in their hatred of the flesh ungratefully yearn to be free from marital arrangement and participation in decent food. They are ignorant and irreligious. Their self-control is irrational....For instance, the Brahmans do not eat meat or drink wine. They despise death and set no value on life, believing in reincarnation. They worship Heracles and Pan as gods. The so-called Holy Men of India also live out their lives in a state of nudity.[5]

Clement seems to posit a link between the Gnostic practices that he sought to condemn and those of Jaina, Buddhist, and Hindu renouncers in India.

The Manichaean religion, with its recognition of Buddha, Zoroaster, Hermes, Plato, and Jesus as primary teachers, taught the opposition of Light and Darkness and required a strict vegetarian diet. Its founder, a Persian called Mani, began preaching in 242 C.E. and was crucified in 276. St. Augustine of Hippo had been a Manichaean for nine years, before turning to Christianity. His disdain for fleshy temptation, perhaps influenced by his Manichaean phase, helped shape his concepts of sin, self, and redemption, though Augustine later rejected the fundamental Manichaean notion that desire can be overcome through one's own efforts, a precept shared with the renouncer traditions of India. Although the influence of Manicheanism waned in Europe by the sixth century,[6] it persisted in Chinese Turkestan at least until the tenth century and provided an easy label by which later similar "heresies" could be condemned by church authorities.

Movements that emphasized self-purity and vegetarianism continued in Europe until the fifteenth century. Paul of Samosata, an Armenian, whose followers were known as Paulicians, taught a doctrine of human perfectibility in the third century. A tenth-century Bulgarian priest named Bogomil established a church with similar teachings that insisted on abstention from both wine and meat. This church rejected water baptism and veneration of the cross. It flourished in both Bulgaria and Macedonia, and also spread into Bosnia, where its followers were called Paterenes.[7]

In the 1140s a movement emerged in Italy known as the Cathar Church, the church of the "pure," the founding of which has been linked to cloth merchants who introduced Bogomil ideas from the Balkan peninsula.[8] By the end of the twelfth century it had spread also to France, Germany, and England. The Cathars, also known as Albigensians, taught a complex, docetist theology that denounced the material world as the work of the devil and disavowed most of the Old Testament. According to the Cathars, the purpose of human life was to purify the soul through chastity and vegetarianism, thereby avoiding reincarnation and attaining release. The killing of animals was forbidden because animals were said to possess a soul; meat, eggs, and milk were all forbidden because they arose from the sinful act of sexual intercourse.[9] They divided their followers into the Believers and the Perfect. The Perfect, who could be male or female, essentially had achieved a divinized state, and were worshipped by the Believers.[10] The Cathars fasted frequently and occasionally encouraged sick members to embark on a fast unto death, known as the Endura.[11] In the thirteenth century, many French nobility embraced the Cathar sect, most notably Count Raymond of Toulouse. The Inquisition, however, set out to destroy the renegade church. Two hundred Perfects were burned without trial at Montsegur in 1238, and in 1243 and 1244 many nobility perished similarly. In 1326, the "last Cathar in France, Limosus Niget, was burned."[12] In 1412, fifteen Cathars were burned to death in Chieri, Italy.[13] These traditions, from the Gnostics and Manichaeans to the Bogomils and the Cathars, bear similarities to Jainism, especially in their emphasis on the purgation of evil through asceticism and their practice of vegetarianism.[14]

Nonviolent Christian attitudes were kept alive by the followers of St. Francis of Assisi, who was probably influenced by the Cathars but managed to legitimize kindness to animals in a theologically acceptable manner.[15] Until a few decades ago, Roman Catholics abstained from eating meat on Fridays, and, in general, Christian monastic fare includes a minimal consumption of meat. Many Christian monastic orders practice total vegetarianism, including the Cistercians (Trappists), the Camaldolese, and the Carthusians. Many members of the Seventh Day Adventist Church, which was founded in Upstate New York by Ellen White in the mid-1800s, practice vegetarianism. The Adventists base their diet on the Biblical passage in which God proclaims "I give you all plants that bear seed everywhere on earth, and every tree bearing fruit which yields seed: they shall be yours for food" (Genesis I:19). The Seventh Day Adventist diet has been hailed by the medical community as a model for good health.[16]

With the rise of colonialism and the increase of trade between Europe and Asia beginning in the sixteenth century, avenues were reopened for direct intercultural contact. Though in the beginning the Europeans were more interested in obtaining Eastern material goods than in learning the complexities of Asian thought and cultures, Asian ideas slowly began to filter westward. During the nineteenth century, the American Transcendentalists were avid readers of the newly published English translations of Sanskrit texts. Ralph Waldo Emerson owned and read copies of the Vedas, the *Laws of Manu*, the Upaniṣads, the *Vishnu Purāṇa*, and the *Bhagavad Gītā*, as well as the Confucian classics. Thoreau said of himself that he knew the scriptures of the Hindus, Chinese, and Persians better than that of the Hebrews. Of the Vedas, Thoreau said:

> There is no grander conception of creation anywhere. It is peaceful as a dream...It is such a beginning and ending as the morning and evening, for they had learned that God's methods are not violent.[17]

Emerson's concept of the all-pervasive, transcendent, Over-soul, of which he said "All that you call the world is the shadow of that substance which you are, the perpetual creation of the powers of thought, of those that are dependent and of those that are independent of your will," closely parallels the Hindu notions of Brahman that underly the practice of nonviolence.[18]

Thoreau's retreat to Walden Pond can be likened to the yogi's renunciation of the world: "Depend upon it that, rude and careless as I am, I would fain practice the yoga faithfully...To some extent, and at rare intervals, even I am a yogin."[19] Thoreau sought to avoid unnecessary violence; in this he shared the underlying practice common to Hinduism, Jainism, Buddhism, and Taoism.[20] In both men's work a passionate love for human justice and the natural order are in evidence, put into action by Thoreau through passive resistance against tyranny and a minimal consumption of natural resources. The power of the hermit filled Emerson with a great optimism, indicating that renouncer values, in his estimation, would ultimately prevail:

> Soon these improvements and mechanical inventions will be superseded; these modes of living lost out of memory; these cities rotted, ruined by war, by new inventions, by new seats of trade, or the geological changes...But the thought which these few hermits strove to proclaim by silence as well as by speech, not only by what they did, but what they forebore to do, shall abide in beauty and strength, to reorganize themselves in nature, to invest themselves anew in other, perhaps higher endowed and happier mixed clay than ours, in fuller union with the surrounding system.[21]

These prophetic words seem to stand as precursors to current ecological thinking.

Renewed interest in Asian culture occurred in the United States during the World Parliament of Religions at Chicago in 1893 and again in the middle of the twentieth century. Gandhi electrified the American press with his Thoreau-like peaceful revolution. After World War II, as well as during the Korean and Vietnam wars, numerous servicemen became acquainted with the philosophies and cultures of Asia, especially Buddhism. Literary figures such as Jack Kerouac, Alan Ginsberg, and Gary Snyder introduced Asian notions to popular American culture beginning in the late 1950s. The 1965 Immigration Act abolished the exclusion of Asians that began in 1882 and had been strengthened in 1924. This allowed an influx of Asians into the United States, including many Asian teachers of the Hindu, Jaina, and Buddhist traditions.

The Jaina notion that life forms are sacred and merit preservation has exerted direct influence on Indian and Asian cultures. Concrete examples are found in the Jaina establishment of animal sanctuaries, the Buddhist practice of releasing animals from certain harm, and in vegetarianism, primarily in India and among Chinese Buddhist monks. With the rise of the animal rights and environmental movements, similar activities are now becoming popular in the United States, supported by new ways of thinking. Christian theologian Jay B. McDaniel has advanced a theology of reverence for life based on post-patriarchal, ecological values, writing that

> the life well lived is one that is open to the divine Heart. Openness of this sort is faith, and it is an art rather than a science. It involves trust in a Presence who cannot be manipulated through conscious control and whose depths cannot be fully exhausted by conceptual formulas or religious doctrines. The fruits of openness include value-pluralistic thinking, care for others, a hunger for justice, the enjoyment of relational power, a union of thought and feeling, discovery of one's self as creatively integrative, and appreciation of nature as organic and evolutionary, and a reverence for life.[22]

This interpretation of the purpose of theology accords easily with the Jaina pronouncements of Acharya Tulsi: in order for life as we know it to survive, we must examine our own individual lifestyles and make changes accordingly.

The principle of noninjury to life is now being newly formulated and justified not according to traditional Jaina cosmology or Buddhist compassion or the Hindu vision of oneness, but according to natural law and individual rights theory as adapted by Thoreau, Gandhi, Martin Luther King, Peter Singer, and Tom Regan, and the ecologically-minded theologians. Just as Jaina multiplicity, Hindu monism, and Buddhist emptiness have all been legitimately employed as rationalizations for the practice of *ahiṃsā*, so now Western philosophical and theological perspectives are justifying and advocating the reversal of harm to both the elemental and animal spheres.

Quite often it is assumed that ethics proceeds from philosophy or theology, that the superiority of a philosophical or theological system results in a superior system of ethics. However, given the shared biology common to the human condition, it stands to reason that a shared ethic would be more palatable to diverse cultures than would be a shared ideology. This is perhaps a nonpatriarchal, ecofeminist approach in the sense that it accounts for many sides of the same issue simultaneously, as does the thought of Catherine Keller, which follows a similar path emphasizing interrelatedness and interpenetration. She writes that:

> We can no more immobilize the divine element in the universe in the form of a single name, a single sex, a single code, creed or cult, than we can freeze the fluid transformations of the universe. A postpatriarchal perspective, expressing a self that is many in one, learns a limpid, diversifying discernment of all things dancing as many in one. But all things do not add up to a deity. Any simple pantheism, deifying the universe, might squelch profound possibilities of relation. For in community, in the matrix of interconnections private and public, we encounter a holiness of Self and Other that is irreducible to any one self or any one other. It has life—lives—of its own...Any being in the universe can be its metaphor.[23]

The process of nonviolent behavior necessitates a dialogical relationship between self and other, human and nature, human and animal, not unlike the reciprocal model proposed by various feminist thinkers. Rather than dominating animals, nature, and other persons as in traditional "patriarchies," the nonviolent world view advocates a noninjurious mode of interaction wherein the things of the world are not regarded as different from oneself. One is reminded of the Chipko movement in India in which women resist the onslaught of harmful logging operations by hugging trees in successful protest against bulldozers and chainsaws, proclaiming the trees to be none other than their very selves.

A world view based on the practice of *ahiṃsā* invites the reconsideration of certain modernist assumptions. The usefulness of a two-valued logic has been deemed questionable. As Nietzsche noted, "What is done out of love always occurs beyond good and evil."[24] Our inspirations are fraught with multiplicities and ambiguities. Arguments for the supremacy of human comfort at the expense of the natural order have proven to be specious and self-contradictory. Animals are part of the same life continuum. The earth can no longer be objectified and manipulated for purposes of human consumerism. The self is not isolable from other selves nor from the larger life order, nor is its mechanistic prolongation necessarily desirable. The multivalent logic of the Jainas, with its sevenfold assessment of reality, provides a paradigm sufficiently flexible and probing for today's issues. Despite its elasticity, it is not merely a logic that justifies relativism, as shown by its initial and pervasive commitment to the doctrine of nonviolence.

The definition and delimitation of the living self in the modern American era has been shaped not by place but by things. Persons do not identify themselves with a particular home town or village or climate or even region; they define and habituate themselves according to degree of economic wealth. Symptoms abound of this syndrome: the boom of the mini-storage industry in America, the rise of the three-car garage as a standard feature of suburban life; the proliferation of electronic gizmos such as video cassette recorders, compact disc players, microwave ovens, trash compacters, telephone answering machines, car phones, and intangible services such as call-waiting and call-forwarding and off-site computer links. The modern, consumerist human being is now defined by the quantity of one's accumulations and one's ability to manipulate them, in contrast to the nonviolent model in which the prime value is found in sloughing off possessions to expose the living self as unfettered energy, consciousness, and bliss. By minimizing the stuff that surrounds and limits the self, a freedom within life emerges.

Today a pressing issue of global proportions has joined countries of all continents in a quest for a common solution. The spectre of environmental ravage looms equally over the Americas, Asia, Africa, and Europe. The technological trance foisted upon the world first in the guise of colonialism and then in the name of development has sired ugly, misshapen children in the form of toxic industrial waste, genetic damage, and psychic despair, as evidenced most notably in Chernobyl and Bhopal. During its earliest appearance in eighteenth-century England, the visionary poet William Blake lamented the oppression and pollution of the factory. A century later, Henry David Thoreau complained of the clamour and smoke in his native Massachusetts. And in the twentieth century, Mahatma Gandhi wrote, as noted earlier, that gods cannot inhabit a land made "hideous by smoke" with crowded roadways filled with rushing cars and people who do not know what they are about.

Personal transformation through the practice of nonviolence can serve not only as a means to improve oneself, but also can help improve society and the world. This idea and its related practice of nonpossession or *aparigraha* apparently affected the American thinker Henry David Thoreau, whose essay, "Walden," has profoundly influenced American attitudes toward our landscape and has inspired generations of naturalists and conservationists, those who in today's parlance are referred to collectively as environmentalists. The affinity and respect for life forms felt in the Indian context resonates with the love of nature so prevalent in the American folk sensibility.[25]

Conclusion

From the material we have surveyed, respect for life as expressed through the ethic of *ahiṃsā* is supported by diverse cosmologies. The Jainas practice nonviolence because all things have life force and all life is sacred. The Hindus practice nonviolence because all life is seen as fundamentally one, part of the same sacred substance that Emerson called Over-soul. In Buddhism, life is to be cherished because it is not permanent; nothing has an abiding self-identity and hence, almost paradoxically, one must have compassion for all beings. The idea of nonviolence is based on a perception of sameness amongst human beings, and between humans and the natural world.

For the first few million years of human existence, nature was providential and mysterious. Since the rise of science and technology it has become commoditized and manipulated. Our comforts have been gained at great expense to all life forms: countless peoples have been displaced by its advances; countless species become extinct each year; the earth itself is burning and groaning.

Yet all is not lost. In addition to boasting an opposable thumb and an ability to communicate using complex languages, human beings above all else are adaptable. Humans have demonstrated that they can live compassionately and tolerantly, particularly when inspired by those moments when the sanctity of life is made real, those moments, however rare they may be, when individuals experience the bliss and momentary fulfillment that comes from an encounter with the sacredness of nature, perceived in nonviolent receptivity to it. Many of us have been filled with feelings of awe such as I experienced at the age of seven or eight when my father and I hiked across several meadows and through hedgerows into virgin forest, where, towering fifty or sixty feet above our heads in a lightning-seared maple tree we saw a huge mass of gleaming honeycomb, oozing honey and reverberating with the hum of thousands of bees. It is an image I will never forget. Such encounters with the beauty of nature are also found in literature, in the romantic poets, in D. H. Lawrence, and in the writings of Emerson and Thoreau. The conservationist John Muir also reflected deeply on the sanctity of nature. In his remarks that follow, the wild bear serves as a symbol for all that is to be found sacred in our shared realities:

> ...Bears are made of the same dust as we, and breathe the same winds and drink of the same waters. A bear's days are warmed by the same sun, his dwellings are over-domed by the same blue sky, and his life turns and ebbs with heart-pulsings like ours...[26]

Through the adoption of an expanded nonviolent ethic, there is some hope for the survival of that marvelous bear, some glimmer on the horizon for the survival of our beleagered planet, some cause for optimism regarding our own lives.

Notes

Chapter 1. Origins and Traditional Articulations of Ahiṃsā

1. See Herman W. Tull, *The Vedic Origins of Karma: Cosmos as Man in Ancient Indian Myth and Ritual* (Albany, New York: State University of New York Press, 1989), especially pages 22–43; and Christopher Chapple, *Karma and Creativity* (Albany, New York: State University of New York Press, 1986), chapter 1.

2. See Ariel Glucklich, *Religious Jurisprudence in the Dharmaśāstra* (New York: MacMillan, 1988).

3. *Ācārāṅga Sūtra* I. 1. 2, I. 5. 5, as excerpted and translated by Nathmal Tatia, *Studies in Jaina Philosophy* (Banaras: Jain Cultural Research Society, 1951), p. 18.

4. Ludwig Alsdorf, *Beiträge zur Geschichte von Vegetarismus und Rinderverehrung in Indien* (Wiesbaden: Verlag der Akademie der Wissenchaften und der Literature in Mainz, 1962).

5. Hanns-Peter Schmidt, "The Origin of Ahiṃsā" in *Mélanges d'Indianisme à la mémoire de Louis Renou* (Paris: Publications de l'Institut de Civilisation Indienne, 1968), p. 626.

6. H. R. Kapadia, "Prohibition of Flesh-Eating in Jainism" in *Review of Philosophy and Religion* (IV, 1933), pp. 232 ff. Kapadia claims that the words meat and fish in the *Ācārāṅga Sūtra* can be interpreted as referring to types of fruits. Furthermore, he cites personal correspondence from Herman Jacobi to Motilal Ladhaji wherein Jacobi refutes his earlier translation that describes monks accepting food with bones.

7. Schimdt, op. cit., p. 627.

8. Hermann Jacobi, *Jaina Sutras Translated from the Prakrit.* Part I. *The Ākārānga Sūtra* and *The Kalpa Sūtra* (Oxford: Clarendon Press, 1884), p. xliii.

9. Unto Tahtinen, *Ahiṃsā: Nonviolence in Indian Tradition* (London: Ryder and Company, 1976).

10. Carlo della Casa, "Ahiṃsā: Significato e Ambito Originari della Non Violenza," in *Indologica Taurinensia* (Volume III, Number 4, 1975–76), pp. 187–196.

11. Peter Schreiner, "Gewaltlosigkeit und Tötungverbot in Hinduismus," in *Angst und Gewalt: Ihre Präsenz und ihre Bewältigung in den Religionen*, edited by Heinrich von Stietencron (Dusseldorf: Patmos Verlag, 1979), pp. 287–308.

12. Koshelya Walli, *The Conception of Ahiṃsā in Indian Thought According to Sanskrit Sources* (Varanasi: Bharata Manisha, 1974).

13. See chapter 4 ("Vedic Apologetics, Ritual Killing, and Foundations of Ethics") in *Tradition and Reflection: Explorations in Indian Thought* by Wilhelm Halbfass (Albany, New York: State University of New York Press, 1991) and his *Studies in Kumārila and Śaṅkara* (Reinbek: Verlag für Orientalistische Fachpublikationen, 1983).

14. Asko Parpola, "Religion Reflected in the Iconic Signs of the Indus Script: Penetrating into the Long Forgotten Picto + Graphic Messages" in *Visible Religion* (VI, 1988), p. 114.

15. Doris Srinivasan, "The So-Called Proto-Śiva Seal from Mohenjo-Daro: An Iconological Assessment" in *Archives of Asian Art*, Vol. 29 (1975–76), p. 57.

16. See Thomas McEvilley, "An Archaeology of Yoga," in *RES*, No. 1 (1981), pp. 44–77.

17. Colin Renfrew, *Archeology and Language: The Puzzle of Indo-European Origins* (Cambridge: Cambridge University Press, 1987).

18. Renfrew, p. 196. Subhash Kak, furthermore, has suggested that the script found on the seals is in fact related to the Brahmi script later used to transcribe Sanskrit. (Subhash Kak, "On the Chronology of Ancient India," *Indian Journal of History of Science*, vol. 22, no. 3 (1987), pp. 222–234.)

19. McEvilley, op. cit., p. 51. It should also be noted that practitioners

of Hatha Yoga imitate animals through various postures, including the lion pose, the cobra pose, etc.

20. *Ācārāṅga Sūtra* II:15:21, in Jacobi, op. cit., p. 197.

21. Jyotindra Jaina and Eberhard Fischer, *Jaina Iconography: The Tīrthaṅkara* (Leiden, 1978), p. 12, as quoted in McEvilley, op. cit.

22. *Ācārāṅga Sūtra* II:15:25, in Jacobi, op. cit., p. 201. *Kalpa Sūtra* 120, in Jacobi, p. 263.

23. Padmanabh S. Jaini provided this information.

24. McEvilley, op. cit., p. 51. See also Heinrich Zimmer, *The Art of India*, Vol. I (New York: Pantheon Books), p. 59.

25. McEvilley, op. cit., p. 52. It perhaps should be noted that U. P. Shah, in his article "Beginnings of Jaina Iconography," *Bulletin of Museums and Archaelogy in Uttar Pradash* (Number 9, 1972), claims these materials do not establish Jaina antiquity.

26. See Katherine Anne Harper, *The Iconography of the Saptamātrikās: Seven Hindu Goddesses of Spiritual Transformation* (Lewiston, New York: The Edwin Mellen Press, 1989), pp. 3–11.

27. Richard Lannoy, *The Speaking Tree: A Study of Indian Culture and Society* (New York: Oxford University Press, 1971), p. 10, plates 7 and 35.

28. Padmanabh S. Jaini, *The Jaina Path of Purification* (Berkeley, California: University of California Press, 1979), p. 33.

29. Madeleine Biardeau, as quoted in Louis Dummont, *Homo Hierarchicus: The Caste System and Its Implications* (Chicago: The University of Chicago Press, 1970), p. 148.

30. As given in Koshelya Walli, op. cit.

31. "The pure minded, who thus confines the extent of his activities, practices absolute *ahiṃsā* for that time by renouncing all himsa possible in the vast space which has been given up." *Puruṣārthasiddhyupāya*, translated by Ajit Prasada (Lucknow: Central Jaina Publishing House, 1933), p. 140.

32. Jaini, op. cit., p. 171.

33. *Ācārāṅga Sūtra* I. 1, in *Jaina Sūtras*, translated from Prakrit by Hermann Jacobi (Delhi: Motilal Banarsidass, 1973; first published by Oxford University Press, 1884). Hereafter referred to as *Ācārāṅga Sūtra*.

34. *Ācārāṅga Sūtra*, I. 1. 3.

35. *devopahāravyājena yajñavayājena ye 'thavā*
ghanti jantūn gataghṛṇā ghorāṃ te yanti durgatim
Yogaśāstra of Hemacandra, II. 39.

36. *Gommaṣṭasāra-Jīvakāṇḍa*, pp. 191–193, as quoted Jaini, op. cit., p. 109.

37. This collection of stories is retold by Padmanabh S. Jaini in his article "Indian Perspectives on the Spirituality of Animals," *Buddhist Philosophy and Culture: Essays in Honour of N. A. Jayawickrema*, edited by David J. Kalupahana and W. G. Weeraratne (Colombo, Sri Lanka: N. A. Jayawickrema Felicitation Volume Committee, 1987), pp. 169–178.

38. Jagmanderlal Jaini, *The Outlines of Jainism* (Cambridge: Cambridge University Press, 1916), p. 47.

39. For a complete list of these 148, see Helmuth von Glasenapp, *The Doctrine of Karman in Jain Philosophy* (Bombay: Bai Vijibai Jivanlal Panalal Charity Fund, 1942), pp. 6–19.

40. Jaini, *The Jaina Path of Purification*, p. 144.

41. Ibid., p. 149.

42. See Jagmanderlal Jaini, op. cit., pp. 48–52 and 105–107.

43. As quoted in Schmidt, op. cit., pp. 652–655.

44. Francis Zimmerman, *The Jungle and the Aroma of Meats: An Ecological Theme in Hindu Medicine* (Berkeley: University of California Press, 1987). See especially chapter VII: "Vegetarianism and Nonviolence."

45. Louis Dumont, *Homo Hierarchicus: The Caste System and Its Implications*, tr. Mark Sainsbury (Chicago: The University of Chicago Press, 1970), p. 149. See also Brian K. Smith, "Eaters, Food, and Social Hierarchy in Ancient India: A Dietary Guide to a Revolution of Values," *Journal of the American Academy of Religion* (Volume LVIII, Number 2, pp. 177–205).

46. Translation by the author.

47. See Bhasker Anand Saletore, *Medieval Jainism: With Special Reference to the Vijayanagara Empire* (Bombay: Karnatak Publishing House, 1938), pp. 269–271.

48. Ashirbadi Lal Srivastava, *Akbar the Great, Volume I: Political History, 1542–1605 A.D.* (Agra: Shiva Lal Agarwala, 1962), p. 264.

49. Ibid, p. 256.

50. Abul Fazl, *Akbar Nama*, tr. H. Beveridge (Calcutta: Asiatic Society of Bengal, 1897), Vol. III, pp. 333–334.

51. Sarvepalli Radhakrishnan, tr., *A Source Book in Indian Philosophy* (Princeton, New Jersey: Princeton University Press, 1957), p. 292.

Chapter 2. Nonviolence, Buddhism, and Animal Protection

1. Lambert Schmithausen, *Buddhism and Nature* (Tokyo: The International Institute for Buddhist Studies, 1991), pp. 4–10. I am grateful to John Taber of the University of New Mexico for sharing this resource with me.

2. *Mahāvagga* I. 78. 4, in *Vinaya Texts*, translated from Pali by T. W. Rhys-Davids and Hermann Oldenberg (Delhi, Motilal Banarasidass, 1974; first published at Oxford University Press, 1882).

3. *Mahāvagga in Vinaya Texts*, III. 1.1.

4. James P. McDermott, "Animals and Humans in Early Buddhism," *Indo-Iranian Journal* (Vol. 32, No. 2, 1989), p. 269.

5. Ibid., p. 274.

6. Ibid., p. 270.

7. Padmanabh S. Jaini, "Indian Perspectives on the Spirituality of Animals," op. cit., p. 171.

8. Ibid., p. 172–173.

9. Ibid., p. 173.

10. Har Dayal, *The Bodhisattva Doctrine in Buddhist Sanskrit Literature* (London: Kegan Paul, 1931) p. 187.

11. "Animals," in *Enclyclopedia of Buddhism*, edited by G. P. Malalasekara (Government Press, Ceylon, 1965), Fascicle 4, pp. 667–672.

12. Dayal, op. cit., p. 182.

13. Jātaka Tale 18, retold from H. T. Francis and E. J. Thomas, *Jataka Tales* (Cambridge: Cambridge University Press, 1916), pp. 20–22.

14. "Rock Edict I," as translated in *Aśoka's Edicts* by Amulyachandra Sen (Calcutta, The Institute of Indology, 1956), p. 64. Hereafter referred to as *Aśoka's Edicts*.

15. "Rock Edict II," *Aśoka's Edicts*, p. 66.

16. "Pillar Edict II," *Aśoka's Edicts*, p. 146.

17. "Pillar Edict V," *Aśoka's Edicts*, pp. 154–156.

18. See D. Seyfort Ruegg, "Ahiṃsā and Vegetarianism in the History of Buddhism," in *Festschrift for Walpola Rahula*, ed. Somaratna Balasooriya and others (London: Gordon Fraser, and Sri Lanka: Vimamsa, 1980); also James P. McDermott, op. cit.

19. Victor H. Mair, *Painting and Performance: Chinese Picture Recitation and Its Indian Genesis* (Honolulu: University of Hawaii Press, 1988).

20. Ibid., p. 51.

21. Ruegg, op. cit.

22. According to D. T. Suzuki, this chapter is probably a later accretion to the text.

23. ...*anene dhīrgenādhvanā saṃsaratām prāṇināṃ nāstyasau kaścit-sattvaḥ sulbharūpo yo na mātābhūtpītā vā bhrātā va bhaginī va putro vā duhitā vānytarānyatro vā svajanabandhabandhūbhūto vā tasyānyajanmaparivṛttāśra-yasya mṛgapaśupakṣiyonyantarbhūtasya bandhorbandūbhūtasya....*

24. Daisetz Teitaro Suzuki, translator, *The Laṅkāvatāra Sūtra* (London: Routledge and Kegan Paul, 1932), p. 216.

25. Ibid., pp. 216–217.

26. Ibid., p. 219.

27. Ibid., p. 220.

28. Ibid., p. 221.

29. Ibid.

30. Dayal, op. cit., p. 199.

31. Dayal, op. cit., p. 199.

32. Dayal, op. cit., p.175.

33. *The Buddha Speaks the Brahma Net Sūtra*, translated by Dharma Realm Buddhist University (Talmage, California: Buddhist Text Translation Society, 1981), p. 150.

34. M. W. deVisser, *Ancient Buddhism in Japan: Sūtras and Ceremonies*

in Use in the Seventh and Eighth Centuries A.D. and their History in Later Times (Leiden: E. J. Brill, 1935), p. 198.

35. George W. Clarke, "The Yü-Li or Precious Records," in *Journal of the China Branch of the Royal Asiatic Society* (New Series, Volume XXVIII, 1893–94, published in Shanghai, 1898), p. 259.

36. Ibid., p. 284.

37. deVisser, op. cit., pp. 198–212.

38. Holmes Welch, *The Practice of Chinese Buddhism, 1900–1950.* (Cambridge, Massachusetts: Harvard University Press, 1967), pp. 378–382.

39. Philip Kapleau, "Animals and Buddhism," *Zen Bow Newsletter: A Publication of the Zen Center* (Vol. V, No. 2, spring, 1983), pp. 1–9. See also his *To Cherish All Life: A Buddhist Case for Becoming Vegetarian* (San Francisco: Harper and Row, 1982).

40. Michael Freeman, "Sung," in *Food in Chinese Culture: Anthropological and Historical Perspectives*, edited by K. C. Chang (New Haven: Yale University Press, 1977), p. 164.

41. Kenneth Ch'en, "Anti-Buddhist Propaganda During the Nan-Ch'ao" in *Harvard Journal of Asiatic Studies*, Vol. 15, Nos. 1 and 2 (1952), pp. 166–192.

42. As quoted in Ch'en, ibid., p. 178.

43. Ibid., p. 180.

44. Ibid., p. 191.

45. Edwin O. Reischauer, *Ennin's Travels in T'ang China* (New York, 1955), p. 222.

46. William LaFleur, "Bones of Contention: Han Yü versus the Buddhists," unpublished manuscript, p. 26.

47. William R. LaFleur, *Buddhism* (Englewood Cliffs, New Jersey: Prentice Hall, 1988), p. 57.

48. Jacques Gernet, *China and the Christian Impact: A Conflict of Cultures* (Cambridge: Cambridge University Press and Paris: Éditions de la Maison des Sciences de l'Homme, 1985), p. 78.

49. Donald E. Gjertson, *Ghosts, Gods, and Retribution: Nine Buddhist Miracle Tales from Six Dynasties and Early T'ang China* (Amherst, Massachu-

setts: International Area Studies Programs, University of Massachusetts at Amherst, 1978), pp. 14–15.

50. Karl S. Y. Kao, editor, *Classical Chinese Tales of the Supernatural and the Fantastic: Selections from the Third to the Tenth Century* (Bloomington, Indiana: Indiana University Press, 1985), pp. 166–171.

51. Ibid, pp. 266–269.

52. Stephen F. Teiser, draft version of "The Growth of Purgatory," p. 13, forthcoming in *Religion and Society in T'ang and Sung China*, eds. Patricia Buckley Ebrey, Peter N. Gregory (Honolulu: University of Hawaii Press, 1993).

53. Clarke, op. cit., p. 309.

54. Ibid., p. 310.

55. Ibid., p. 324.

56. Ibid., p. 335.

57. Ibid., p. 395.

58. Donald E. Gjertson, "Rebirth as an Animal in Medieval Chinese Buddhism" *Bulletin of the Society for the Study of Chinese Religions* (Vol. 8, 1980), pp. 56–69.

59. Raghu Vira, *Chinese Poems and Pictures on Ahiṃsā* (Nagpur: International Academy of Indian Culture, 1954), p. 1.

60. Ibid., p. 2.

61. Ibid., p. 4.

62. Donald Griffin, *Animal Thinking* (Cambridge, Massachusetts: Harvard University Press, 1984).

63. Raghu Vira, op. cit., p. 8.

64. Ibid., p. 70.

65. Ibid., p. 78.

66. Ibid., p. 1.

67. In conversation during a seminar entitled "Buddhism and Culture in China and Japan" sponsored by the National Endowment for the Humanities at the University of California, Los Angeles, 1989.

68. Alicia Matsunaga, *The Buddhist Philosophy of Assimilation: The Historical Development of the Honji-Suijaku Theory* (Rutland, Vermont: Charles E. Tuttle, 1969), pp. 160–162.

69. Kyoko Motomochi Nakamura, tr., *Miraculous Stories from the Japanese Buddhist Tradition: The Nihon ryōiki of the Monk Kyōkai* (Cambridge, Massachusetts: Harvard University Press, 1973), p. 117.

70. Ibid., pp. 132–133.

71. Ibid., p. 127.

72. Ibid., pp. 164–166.

73. For statistics on the use of animals in laboratory science, see Richard Ryder, *Victims of Science* (London: Davis-Poynter, 1975). See Peter Singer, *Animal Liberation: A New Ethics For Our Treatment of Animals* (New York, Avon Books, 1975) and Jay B. McDaniel, *Of God and Pelicans: A Theology of Reverence for Life* (Louisville, Kentucky: Westminster/John Knox Press, 1989) for a clear exposition of animal rights from a philosophical and theological perspective, respectively. For an earlier version of this essay, and for a discussion of the treatment of animals in the major religious traditions of the world, see Tom Regan, editor, *Animal Sacrifices: Religious Perspectives on the Use of Animals in Science* (Philadelphia: Temple University Press, 1986).

74. See *Bṛhadāraṇyanka Upaniṣad* I. 1–2.

75. For instance, the *Sāṃkhya Kārikā* of Īśvarakṛṣṇa dismisses Vedic sacrifices as being ineffective means to alleviate suffering because of the destruction they entail. The description of ahiṃsā in Patañjali's *Yoga Sūtra*, similar to that in Jaina texts, condemns violence whether done, caused, or approved, and claims that the Great Vow (*mahāvrata*) is not limited by time, place, or circumstance.

76. Jaini, *The Jaina Path of Purification*, p. 285n.

77. Michael Tobias, *Life Force: The World of Jainism* (Berkeley, California: Asian Humanities Press, 1991), p. 31.

78. For a graphic depiction of an animal shelter in Ahmedabad, see the video *Frontiers of Peace: Jainism in India*, produced by Paul Kueperferle (Mendham, New Jersey: The Visual Knowledge Corporation, 1986). Such shelters are also depicted in *Ahiṃsā: Non-Violence*, a Public Broadcasting Service documentary produced and directed by Michael Tobias in 1987.

79. For a discussion of Buddhist medical practices, see Raoul Birnbaum, *The Healing Buddha* (Boulder, Colorado, Shambhala, 1979).

80. See *The Tibetan Book of the Dead*, translated by W. Y. Evans Wentz (London: Oxford University Press, 1927) and *The Wheel of Death* by Philip Kapleau (New York: Harper & Row, 1971).

81. This story is recounted in the *Ārya-Sarvabuddha-mahārahasy-opāykauśalyajñanottarabodhisattvaparipṛcchāparivarta*, Sūtra 38 in the Mahā-ratnakūta collection. It is translated in Garma C. C. Chang (general ed.), *A Treasury of Mahāyāna Sūtras: Selections from the Mahāratnakūta Sūtra* (University Park, Pennsylvania: Pennsylvania State University Press, 1983), pp. 456–458.

82. Philip Kapleau, *To Cherish All Life: A Buddhist View of Animal Slaughter and Meat Eating* (Rochester, New York: Zen Center, 1981), republished by Harper and Row in 1982.

83. Christopher Stone, *Earth and Other Ethics* (New York: Harper and Row, 1988).

84. Tenzin Gyatso, the fourteenth Dalai Lama, *Universal Responsibility and the Good Heart* (Dharamsala, India: Library of Tibetan Works and Archives, 1980), p. 78.

Chapter 3. Nonviolent Asian Responses to the Environmental Crisis

1. *Ṛg Veda* X:190, 13-14. Translated by Antonio T. DeNicolás in *Meditations Through the Ṛg Veda* (New York: Nicolas Hays, 1976).

2. *Bṛhadāraṇyaka Upaniṣad* III:9.28. Translated by Robert Ernest Hume in *The Thirteen Principal Upaniṣads* (Oxford: Oxford University Press, 1931).

3. Selections are quoted from *Hymns of the Atharva-Veda*, translated by Maurice Bloomfield (Oxford: Oxford University Press, 1897).

4. *Bhagavad Gītā*, V:18.

5. Aldo Leopold, *A Sand County Almanac* (London: Oxford University Press, 1949), p. 207.

6. M. K. Gandhi, *My Socialism* (Ahmedabad: Navajivan Publishing House, 1959), p. 36.

7. Pritam Singh, *Gandhi's Constructive Programme* (Lahore: Paramount Publications, 1944), p. 128.

8. Gandhi, *My Socialism*, pp. 33–34.

9. Louis Fischer, *The Essential Gandhi* (New York: Vintage Books, 1962), p. 327.

10. M. K. Gandhi, *The Village Reconstruction* (Bombay: Bharatiya Vidya Bhavan, 1966), p. 43.

11. Ibid., p. 30.

12. Gandhi, *My Socialism*, pp. 34–35.

13. Ibid., p. 34.

14. E. F. Schumacher, "Buddhist Economics," in *Asia: A Handbook*, edited by Guy Wint (London: Anthony Blond, 1965), p. 699.

15. An analysis of Schumacher vis-à-vis Gandhian principles is found in Glyn Richards, *The Philosophy of Gandhi* (London: Curzon Press, 1982), pp. 124–133.

16. Schumacher, op. cit., p. 699.

17. Michael Tobias, *Life Force: The World of Jainism*, op. cit., pp. 37–39.

18. Kartikeya V. Sarabhai, "Strategy for Environmental Education: An Approach for India," paper presented at the Annual Conference of the North American Association for Environmental Education, Washington, D.C., 1985, p. 12.

19. "Centre for Environment Education Annual Report, 1987–88," Nehru Foundation for Development, Ahmedabad.

20. "The Mohanpur Experiment in Natural Farming: Second Interim Report, June 1988," Gandhi Peace Foundation and The Indian Institute of Technology, Delhi.

21. Information on this movement is included in the periodical publication *Worldwide Women in the Environment*, P.O. Box 40885, Washington, D.C. 20016.

22. Ann Spanel, "Interview with Vandana Shiva," in *Woman of Power* (Vol. 9, 1988), pp. 27–31.

23. Ibid.

24. Ibid., p. 31.

25. Vandana Shiva, *Staying Alive: Women, Ecology, and Development* (London: Zed Books, 1988), p. 6.

26. Mark Fineman, "A River, A Dam, and an Old Man's Last Battle" in *Los Angeles Times*, May 1, 1990, Section H [World Report], p. 1.

27. For a complete biography of Acharya Tulsi, see *Acharya Tulsi: Fifty Years of Selfless Dedication*, edited by R. P. Bhatnagar, S. L. Gandhi, Rajul Bhargava, and Ashok K. Jha (Ladnun, India: Jain Vishva Bharati, 1985).

28. See *Anuvrat Movement: A Constructive Endeavor Towards a Nonviolent Multicultural Society*, edited by S. L. Gandhi (Rajasmand, India: Anuvrat Vishva Bharati, 1987).

29. S. Gopalan, "The Anuvrat Movement," in *Acharya Tulsi: Fifty Years*, op. cit., p. 20.

30. Sarvepalli Radhakrishnan, in *Acharya Tulsi: Fifty Years*, op. cit., Part 4, p. 17.

31. As quoted in William R. LaFleur, "Saigyo and the Buddhist Value of Nature," in *Nature in Asian Traditions of Thought: Essays in Environmental Philosophy*, edited by J. Baird Callicott and Roger T. Ames (Albany, New York: State University of New York Press, 1989), p. 184.

32. William Grosnick, "The Buddhahood of the Grasses and the Trees: Ecological Sensitivity or Scriptural Misunderstanding," presented at the College Theology Society Annual Meeting, Loyola University, New Orleans, 1990, p. 12.

33. Ibid., p. 19.

34. Clarke, "The Yü-Li or Precious Records," p. 336.

35. Ibid., p. 336.

36. Ibid., p. 338.

37. Joan Halifax, "The Third Body: Buddhism, Shamanism, and Deep Ecology," in *Dharma Gaia: A Harvest of Essays in Buddhism and Ecology*, edited by Allan Hunt Badiner (Berekeley, California: Parallax Press, 1990), p. 25.

38. Padmasiri de Silva, "Buddhist Environmental Ethics," in *Dharma Gaia*, op. cit., p. 18.

39. See David Edward Shaner, "The Japanese Experience of Nature," in *Nature in Asian Traditions of Thought*, op. cit., p. 169.

40. Lambert Schmithausen, *Buddhism and Nature* (Tokyo: The International Insitute for Buddhist Studies, 1991), pp. 38–41.

41. Ibid., pp. 26–27.

42. Ibid., p. 53.

43. "Interview with Phra Prachak," *Seeds of Peace* (Vol. 8, No. 1), 1992, p. 32.

44. Ecology Plenary Address by Chatsumarn Kabilsingh, Fourth International Buddhist-Christian Dialogue Conference, Boston University, July 31, 1992.

45. Lynn White, Jr., "The Historic Roots of Our Ecologic Crisis," *Science*, 155 (March 1967).

46. For a discussion of ecological panentheism, see Jay B. McDaniel, *Of God and Pelicans: A Theology of Reverence For Life* (Louisville, Kentucky: Westminster/John Knox Press, 1989) and his forthcoming contribution to *Ecological Prospects*, edited by Christopher Key Chapple (Albany: State University of New York Press).

47. For a history of the development of this idea, see Jacques Grinevald, "Sketch for a History of the Idea of the Biosphere," in *Gaia, the Thesis, the Mechanisms and the Implications*, edited by Peter Bunyard and Edward Goldsmith (Cornwall: Wadebridge Ecological Centre, 1988), pp. 1–34.

48. James Lovelock, "The Gaia Hypothesis," in *Gaia*, op. cit., p. 38.

49. See James E. Lovelock, *Ages of Gaia* (New York: W. W. Norton, 1988).

50. Lynn Margulis, talk delivered at "Ecological Prospects: Theory and Practice," conference at Loyola Marymount University, 1991.

51. See Grinevald, op. cit., pp. 8–12.

52. See Frances Moore Lappe, *Food First: Beyond the Myth of Scarcity* (Boston: Houghton-Mifflin, 1977).

53. See Thomas Berry, *The Dream of the Earth* (San Francisco: Sierra Club Books, 1988).

Chapter 4. Otherness and Nonviolence in the Mahābhārata

1. Jean-Claude Carrière, *The Mahabharata: A Play Based upon the Indian Classic Epic*, translated from the French by Peter Brook (New York: Harper & Row, 1987), p. xii.

2. Ibid., p. 105.

3. Ibid., p. 198.

4. Translation by Christopher Key Chapple of *Mahābhārata* XIII:114, based on the Sanskrit edition by Vishnu S. Sukthankar and others, Fascicule 34 (Poona: Bhandarkar Oriental Research Institute, 1963), pp. 622-623.

5. Carrière, op. cit., p. 151.

6. Ibid., p. 105.

7. *Chāndogya Upaniṣad* VIII. 12, as translated in Robert Ernest Hume, *The Thirteen Principal Upaniṣads* (New York: Oxford University Press, 1930), p. 272.

8. *Yoga Sūtra* IV:17.

9. In the last scene, the principal characters have returned to their "own natures," meaning that Karṇa has gone to the sun, Bhīma to the wind, Draupadī to the goddess Śrī, and so forth. Having attained to this blessed state, they are free from further birth. "Having renounced the body, they have conquered heaven through meritorious word, thought, and deed." See *Mahābhārata* XVIII:4:19.

Chapter 5. Nonviolent Approaches to Multiplicity

1. Jaini, *The Jaina Path*, op. cit., p. 88.

2. The many schools of Vedānta are well aware of "the competition," and Tibetan debate training focuses on learning various Buddhist and non-Buddhist traditions.

3. Within the Upaniṣads, we find a fourfold analysis of reality: waking, dreaming, deep sleep, and the "fourth" state (*turīya*), wherein one identifies with the highest self. See Andrew O. Fort's *The Self and Its States* (Delhi: Motilal Banarsidass, 1990). Nāgārjuna's Madhyāmika school of Mahāyāna Buddhism outlines (and rejects) four "corners" of reality: existence, nonexistence, both existence and nonexistence, neither existence nor nonexistence. See Kenneth Inada's *Nāgārjuna, A Translation of His Mūlamadhyāmika-kārikā with an Introductory Essay* (Tokyo: Hokuseido Press, 1970).

4. Bimal Krishna Matilal, *The Central Philosophy of Jainism (Anekānta-Vāda)* (Ahmedabad: L. D. Institute of Indology, 1981), p. 55.

5. H. R. Kapadia, *Introduction to Haribhadra Sūri's Anekāntajayapatākā*

with His Own Commentary and Municandra Sūri's Supercommentary (Baroda: Oriental Institute, 1947), p. cxviii.

6. Ibid., p. cxiv.

7. F. W. Thomas, *The Flower Spray of the Quodammodo Doctrine: Śrī Mallisenasūri's Syād-Vāda-Mañjari* (Delhi: Motilal Banarsidass, 1958) p. 78.

8. Ibid., p. 128.

9. See my introduction to *The Concise Yogavāsiṣṭha*, excerpted and translated by Swami Venkatesananda (Albany: State University of New York Press, 1984).

10. Paul F. Knitter, *No Other Name? A Critical Survey of Christian Attitudes Toward the World Religions* (Maryknoll, New York: Orbis, 1985).

11. Seyyed Hossein Nasr, *Knowledge and the Sacred* (New York: Crossroad, 1981), p. 289.

12. Ibid., p. 291.

13. Leonard Swidler, editor, *Toward a Universal Theology of Religion* (Maryknoll, New York: Orbis, 1987), pp. 30 and 36.

14. Ibid., p. 122.

15. Paul J. Griffiths, *An Apology for Apologetics: A Study in the Logic of Interreligious Dialogue* (Maryknoll, New York: Orbis Books, 1991).

16. See Gerhard Oberhammer, ed., *Inclusivismus: Eine Indische Denkform* (Vienna: Institute of Indology, University of Vienna, 1983) and Wilhelm Halbfass, *India and Europe* (Albany, New York: State University of New York Press, 1988).

17. Robert N. Minor, *Bhagavad Gītā: An Exegetical Commentary* (New Delhi: Heritage Publishers, 1982), p. xvi.

18. Ibid., pp. xvi–xix.

19. Max Mueller, *The Six Systems of Indian Philosophy* (London: Longmans, Green, and Co., 1928), p. 40.

20. Antonio T. deNicolás, *Avatāra: The Humanization of Philosophy through the Bhagavad Gītā* (New York: Nicolas Hays, 1976), p. 164.

21. Judith A. Berling, *The Syncretic Religion of Lin Chao-en* (New York: Columbia University Press, 1980), p. 9.

22. Erich Frauwallner, *History of Indian Philosophy*, Vol. I, translated by V. M. Bedekar (Delhi: Motilal Banarsidass, 1973), p. 335.

Chapter 6. The Jaina Path of Nonresistant Death

1. Jaini, *The Jaina Path of Purification*, op. cit., p. 180.

2. Katherine K. Young's essay on euthanasia provides an historical survey of Hindu forms of self-willed death, with some references to Jainism. See "Euthanasia: Traditional Hindu Views and the Contemporary Debate," in *Hindu Ethics: Purity, Abortion, and Euthanasia*, Harold G. Coward, Julius J. Lipner, and Katherine K. Young (Albany, New York: State University of New York Press, 1989), pp. 71–130.

3. Yajneshwar S. Shastri, "Place of Suicide in Indian Culture and Religions," *Jain Journal* (Vol. XXII, No. 2), 1987, pp. 39–52.

4. See Kautilya's *Arthaśāstra*, IV:7, translated by R. Shamasastry (Mysore: Wesleyan Missionary Press, 1923).

5. S. Settar, *Inviting Death: An Indian Attitude towards the Ritual Death* (Leiden: E. J. Brill, 1989), p. 131.

6. D. A. Binchy, "Irish History and Irish Law: I," *Studia Hibernia* (Vol. 15), 1975, pp. 7–36.

7. Collete Caillat, "Fasting Unto Death According to the Jaina Tradition," *Acta Orientalia* (Vol. 38, 1977), p. 46.

8. T. K. Tukol, *Sallekhanā Is Not Suicide* (Ahmedabad: L. D. Institute of Indology, 1976), p. 8.

9. Ibid., p. 108.

10. Amṛtacandra, *Puruṣārthasiddhyupāya*, translated by Ajit Prasad (Lucknow: Central Jaina Publishing House, 1933), pp. 71–73, 44.

11. Caillat, op. cit., p. 48.

12. Barnett, L. D., tr., *The Antagaḍa-dasāo and the Aṇuttarovavāiya-dasāo* (London, 1907), p. 57, as quoted in Caillat, op. cit.

13. Ibid.

14. Tukol, op. cit., pp. 20–25.

15. Settar, op. cit., pp. 137–38.

16. Ibid., pp. 139–40.

17. Tukol, op. cit., p. 60.

18. Mrs. Sinclair Stevenson, *The Heart of Jainism*, pp. 163–168, as quoted in Tukol, op. cit., p. 93.

19. Louis Renou, *Religions of Ancient India* (1953), p. 124, as quoted in Jaini, op. cit., p. 232.

20. These include nonviolence, truthfulness, nontheft, fidelity in marriage, limitations on wealth, restricted travel, and so forth. See chapter 1.

21. Katherine K. Young quotes a news article from the Toronto *Globe and Mail* (December 17, 1987) in which the fast unto death of Badri Prasad is said to guarantee him sainthood. She also notes that in spite of legislation against the Hindu practice of *sati*, Indian law seems not to interfere with the Jaina tradition of *sallekhanā*.

22. See "Euthanasia," Pope John Paul II, Declaration of the Sacred Congregation for the Doctrine of the Faith (May 5, 1980), in *On Moral Medicine: Theological Perspectives in Medical Ethics* (Grand Rapids: William B. Eerdmans, 1987), pp. 441–44.

23. Ibid., p. 444.

24. Gerald Kelly, S.J., *Medico-Moral Problems*, p. 62, as quoted in Lisa Sowle Cahill, "A 'Natural Law' Reconsideration of Natural Law," in *On Moral Medicine*, op. cit.

25. B. Srinivasa Murthy, tr., *The Bhagavad Gītā* (Long Beach, California: Long Beach Publications, 1991), II:28, p. 38.

Chapter 7. Living Nonviolence

1. See R. Baine Harris, ed., *Neoplatonism and Indian Thought* (Albany, New York: State University of New York Press, 1982) and Chedomil Velyachich, "Jainism and Early Influences of the Indian Ahimsa Religion in Europe," *Bulletin of the Ramakrishna Mission Institute of Culture* (Vol. XIX, 1968), pp. 1–11.

2. *The Geography of Strabo*, translated by Horace Leonard Jones (New York: G. P. Putnam, 1930), p. 101 [15, I.59].

3. Ibid., p. 103 [15, I.60].

4. Ibid., p. 105 [15, I.60].

5. Ibid, p. 293. [III:60].

6. Jeffrey Burton Russell, *Dissent and Reform in the Early Middle Ages* (Berkeley: University of California Press, 1965), p. 193.

7. Ibid., p. 192.

8. See Russell, p. 192 and Steven Runciman, *The Medieval Manichee: A Study of the Christian Dualist Heresy* (Cambridge: Cambridge University Press, 1982) pp. 118, 169.

9. Russell, pp. 204–6; 209–10.

10. In contrast, the Jainas state that the mendicant Jambhu (d. 463 B.C.E.) was the last person to attain perfection in the current era. See Padmanabh S. Jaini, *Gender and Salvation: Jaina Debates on the Spiritual Liberation of Women* (Berkeley: University of California Press, 1991), p. 98.

11. See Runciman, pp. 158–159; Russell, 1965, 204.

12. Gordon Leff, *Heresy in the Later Middle Ages: The Relation of Heterodoxy to Dissent c. 1250–c. 1450* (New York: Barnes & Noble, 1967), p. 450.

13. Ibid., p. 451.

14. For documentation of vegetarianism in the Manichaean, neo-Manichaean, and Bogomil sects, see Dmitri Obolensky, *The Bogomils: A Study in Balkan Neo-Manichaeism* (Middlesex: Anthony C. Hall, 1948), pp. 19–20, 127–128, 221.

15. Runciman, p. 179.

16. See Gary Land, ed., *Adventism in America: A History* (Grand Rapids, Michigan: William B. Eerdmans, 1986); Anne Devereaux Jordan, *The Seventh Day Adventists: A History* (New York: Hippocrene Books, 1988); and Gerald Carson, *Cornflake Crusade* (New York: Rinehart and Company, 1957).

17. Bradford Torrey and Francis H. Allen, eds., *The Journal of Henry D. Thoreau*, Volume I, (Boston: Houghton Mifflin Company, 1949), p. 276.

18. Ralph Waldo Emerson, *Nature: Addresses and Lectures* (Boston: Houghton Mifflin and Company, 1903), p. 334.

19. Arthur Christy, *The Orient in American Transcendentalism* (New York: Columbia University Press, 1932), p. 201.

20. William Bysshe Stein, *Two Brahman Sources of Emerson and*

Thoreau: Rajah Rammohan Roy and William Ward (Binghamton, New York: SUNY, 1966).

21. Emerson, op. cit., p. 359.

22. Jay B. McDaniel, *Of God and Pelicans: A Theology of Reverence for Life* (Louisville, Kentucky: Westminster/John Knox Press, 1989), p. 144.

23. Catherine Keller, *From a Broken Web: Separation, Sexism, and Self* (Boston: Beacon Press, 1986), p. 250.

24. *Beyond Good and Evil,* 153, as excerpted in *The Portable Nietsche,* edited by Walter Kaufmann (New York: Viking Press, 1954), p. 444.

25. Much of my own interest in nonviolence and the preservation of the earth stems from direct experience with earth processes. I grew up with sunrises on the schoolbus and sunsets over the Genesee River Valley that were shared and discussed in detail with family and neighbors. On Earth Day 1970 we planted several hundred poplar trees on the grounds of my high school in upstate New York, which grew mightily and quickly to a height of fifty or sixty feet. By Earth Day 1990, most of these had become denuded, dead, and dangerous due to the ill effects of acid rain. In California, my life amidst the canyons of Los Angeles County was bulldozed into environmental chaos during the economic boom of the 1980s. The jack rabbits and hawks and owls and skunks encountered during predawn and twilight hikes have been driven from their habitat; biological ecologists tell me that they will not survive elsewhere nor can they return.

26. Stephen Fox, *The American Conservation Movement: John Muir and His Legacy* (Madison, Wisconsin: The University of Wisconsin Press, 1985), p. 374.

Index

27297652R00090

Made in the USA
Lexington, KY
03 November 2013